Seashore Life of the Caribbean

A BEACHCOMBER'S GUIDE

Alick and Sarah Jones

MACMILLAN
CARIBBEAN

Macmillan Education
Between Towns Road, Oxford OX4 3PP
A division of Macmillan Publishers Limited
Companies and representatives throughout the world

www.macmillan-caribbean.com

ISBN 1-4050-0760-5

First published 2005

Designed and typeset by Carol Hulme

Cover design by Gary Fielder at AC Design

Cover photographs by Alick and Sarah Jones

The authors and publishers would like to thank the following for permission to reproduce their photographic material:

Alamy p108; **Corbis** (Peter Johnson) p136, (Lyndia Richardson) p49 (b), (Barry Voight/Pennsylvania University/Reuters) p4; **Alick and Sarah Jones** pp iv, vii, 1, 2, 3, 6, 9(b) 10(t), 12, 13, 14, 16, 18, 21, viii, 26(t, b). 27, 28, 29, 30, 31, 32, 33, 34, 35, 36, 37, 38(t, b), 39, 40, 41, 42, 43, 44, 45, 46(t, b) 47(b), 49(t), 53, 55(t, b), 56(t, b), 58 (b), 59, 61(t, b), 62(t), 63(t, b), 64(b), 65, 66(t, b), 67, 68, 39(t, b), 70, 71, 73(t, b), 74, 75, 76, 77, 78(t, b), 79, 80, 81, 82, 83(t, b), 84, 85(t, b), 86, 88, 89, 90, 91, 92, 93(t, b), 94, 95, 96, 97(t, b), 98, 99(t, b), 100(t, b), 101, 102, 103, 104, 105, 107(t, b), 109, 111, 112, 113, 114, 115(b, inset), 116, 117, 118(t, b), 119, 120 (t, b), 121, 122, 123(t, b), 124, 125, 126(t, b), 127 (b, inset), 128(t, inset), 129(t, b), 130, 131, 132, 133, 134, 138 (t, b), 139 (b, inset), 140, 141, 142, 143, 144(t, b), 145, 146, 147(t, b), 148 (t, b), 149, 152, 155, 157, 158(t, b), 159, 160, 161, 162; **Oxford Scientific Films** p9(t).

Printed and bound in Thailand

2009 2008 2007 2006 2005
10 9 8 7 6 5 4 3 2 1

Dedicated to Hannah, Benjamin and Polly who shared with us our first experiences of the Caribbean

Contents

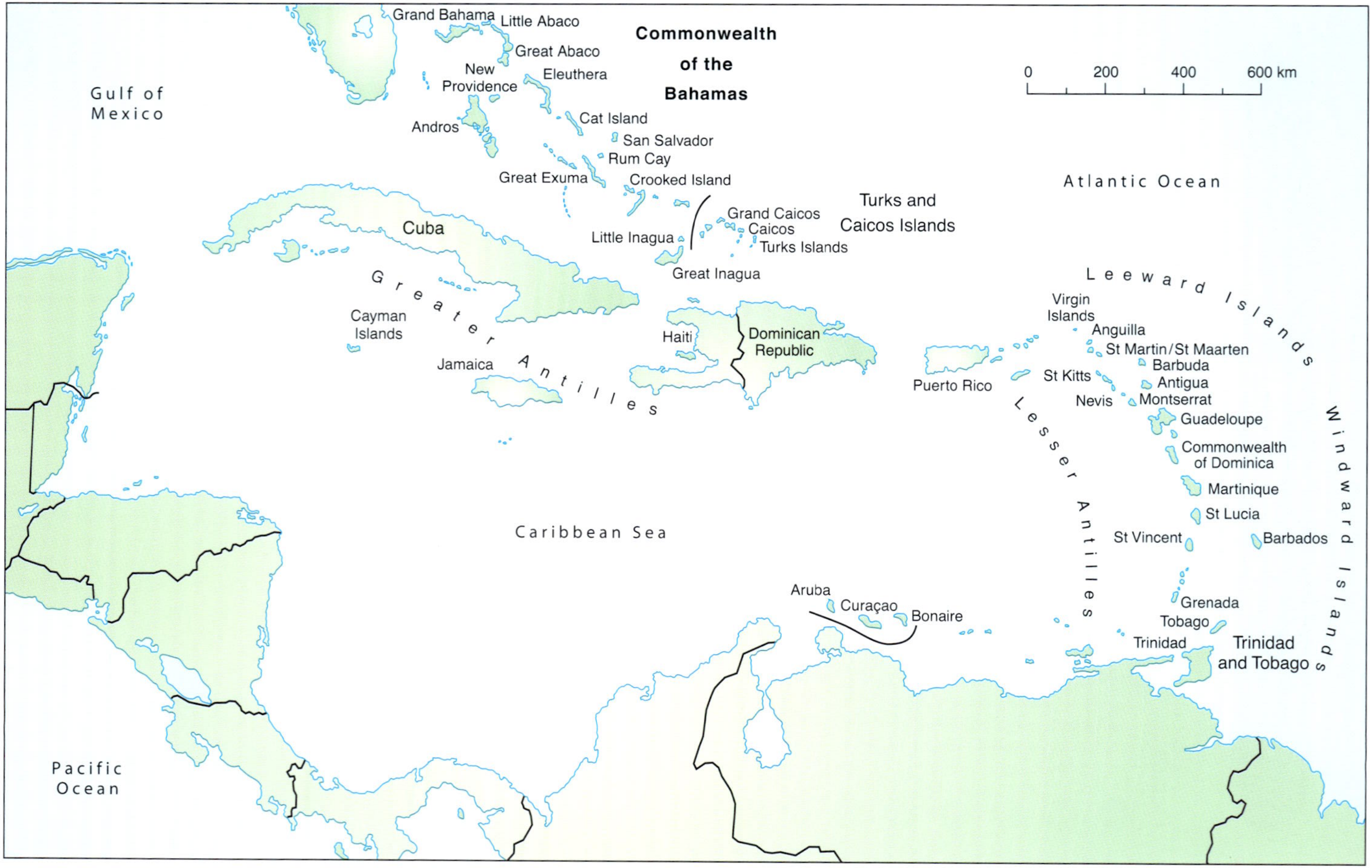
Gulf of Mexico
Grand Bahama
Little Abaco
Great Abaco
New Providence
Eleuthera
Andros
Commonwealth of the Bahamas
Cat Island
San Salvador
Rum Cay
Great Exuma
Crooked Island
0
200
400
600 km
Atlantic Ocean
Turks and Caicos Islands
Grand Caicos
Caicos
Turks Islands
Little Inagua
Great Inagua
Cuba
Greater Antilles
Cayman Islands
Jamaica
Haiti
Dominican Republic
Puerto Rico
Leeward Islands
Virgin Islands
Anguilla
St Martin/St Maarten
Barbuda
St Kitts
Antigua
Nevis
Montserrat
Guadeloupe
Commonwealth of Dominica
Martinique
St Lucia
St Vincent
Barbados
Windward Islands
Lesser Antilles
Grenada
Tobago
Trinidad
Trinidad and Tobago
Aruba
Curaçao
Bonaire
Caribbean Sea
Pacific Ocean

Preface

As always with a project such as this the authors have depended to a considerable extent upon the help, expertise, hospitality and patience of others. Now that we no longer live in the Caribbean this has been particularly true. George Warner, the Director of the Centre for Marine Sciences at the University of the West Indies (UWI), Mona, once more gave us space in his offices and allowed us access to the centre's collection of pamphlets and journals. We stayed for some time with him and Monica on our visits to Jamaica and once again enjoyed their hospitality and company. In Tobago we enjoyed our beachside apartment, courtesy of the ever-congenial Graham and Carole Beckett (and enjoyed Graham's fish catches). In Antigua it was good to renew an old acquaintance with Desmond and Lisa Nicholson and to benefit from their vast experience and wisdom concerning that rapidly changing island. Both Dr Angela Fields (an ex-postgraduate of ARJ's) and Dr Sean Carrington (of the Department of Biological and Chemical Sciences, UWI, Cave Hill, Barbados) helped with their expertise in fauna and flora respectively. Dr David Hicks (of the Center for Coastal and Marine Studies, Beaumont, Texas) supplied information on the introduced green mussel, its spread and pest status within the region. The Library of the Royal Botanic Gardens at Kew gave one of us (SEJ) access to some rare (in the United Kingdom) books. Our thanks go to all of these people and institutions, but needless to say the errors that remain are wholly our responsibility.

1 Introduction

What this book does and does not try to do

Caribbean seashores offer that magic mixture of sun, sand and sparkling sea. To stroll along the beach at sunset with the promise of a rum punch and perhaps a dinner of flying fish to follow does much to calm the agitation of twenty-first century living. But for many beach strollers, swimming and sunbathing, although restful, are not enough. Along the strandline are all sorts of strange and beautiful objects, in particular seashells. On the rocks are unfamiliar snails or sea urchins. A range of exotic birds parade past, and behind the beach grow many characteristic shore plants. Perhaps around the corner of the bay lies the mysterious world of the mangrove swamp. Many Caribbean holidaymakers and residents will feel a need to know more about these things.

Most guides to Caribbean marine life are intended for divers and snorkellers. Those who are interested in the living world of the sea but do not take to the water in either of these ways are not well catered for. We aim to fill that gap with a book designed for those who confine their seashore interests (more or less) to dry land. We hope also that divers and snorkellers (who can't spend *all* day in the water) will be occasionally persuaded to turn their attention to beaches. They will find objects of beauty and fascination which they may have previously neglected in favour of sub-aquatic life.

Fig 1.1 *Beautiful sandy beaches abound in the Caribbean but this book will also deal with beachcombing on other kinds of shores.*

For all people who spend time on Caribbean seashores, we hope this book will enliven their interest in the world around them and stimulate them to look with fresh eyes at the sand, rocks and mud. We also hope it will help them to identify the various things, living and dead, that they will come across. However this book is not intended to be only for identification. Indeed it cannot hope to be an inclusive field guide. There are two main reasons for this. The first is that the range of organisms encountered on seashores is huge and drawn from many very disparate groups; from birds to seaweeds, and lichens to reptiles. To give enough information to identify even the commoner members of these communities would result in a very cumbersome (and most likely rather dull) volume. The second reason is that we are hoping to help readers to gain an insight into how and why seashores are the way they are. This involves saying more about the living biology and ecology of the animals and plants than simply putting a name to them.

Although the Caribbean has a long mainland coast, our book is primarily concerned with the islands and, because of our personal knowledge and experience, the major emphasis is on the English-speaking ones.

What do we mean by 'seashore'?

Seashores are where land and sea meet. For most people living in or visiting the Caribbean this means golden sandy beaches. But there are other such borders, in particular where the land presents the sea with a rocky rather than a sandy margin. Then there are many shores where waves are small and the land behind them is low lying. In such conditions there may well be a swamp dominated by a community of tree species called mangroves. These three, sand, rock and mangrove, will be taken as the major types of seashore for this book. Of course there will be intermediate, mixed and complicated situations but the typical examples are easy to identify.

Fig 1.2 *A surprising number of live animals and plants can be found on rocky shores.*

Fig 1.3 *Mangrove swamps are well worth a visit both because of their own lush beauty and for the range of animals and plants that they contain.*

Having realised that there are various sorts of seashore we must consider where they start and finish; when does seashore become land on one side and sea on the other? This is a less easy question to answer than might seem to be the case at first sight, particularly on the land side. On the seaward side one could define the edge of the seashore as that point below which the rock, sand or mud is always covered by the sea. In this book we have adopted that definition except that occasionally we have referred to shallow-water life that can be easily observed by paddling in a few centimetres of water or looking over the side of a boat or harbour wall. To landward it is easy to observe tide lines of various sorts marking the highest point the sea has reached recently. However, such markers are sometimes misleading. Caribbean beaches are subject to fairly frequent storms and sometimes to hurricanes. Although the latter are mercifully few and far between they leave long-lasting changes to both shorelines and the nearby seabed. Tropical storms that strike more often will change the physical shape of the shoreline and blow sea water tens of metres inshore. Indeed shores facing east and which thus receive the full force of the trade winds will often be subjected to wind-borne spray for many months of the year. The salt carried in this spray may have a profound effect on the vegetation for quite a distance inland. Similarly, waves breaking on rocks will send spray far above the normal high tide mark perhaps allowing marine snails to survive high up above sea level.

Taking the above into consideration we will generally consider animals and plants (and their remains) that occur between the lowest point on the beach that is ever uncovered by the sea and the highest point that is splashed by spray during stormy weather. Additionally, we will include some trees, shrubs or herbs that can cope with beachside conditions and which are often characteristic of plant communities just behind beaches.

The Caribbean region and its climate

The Caribbean Sea lies entirely within the tropics, between 27°N and 8°N; the Tropic of Cancer passes just north of Cuba. The sea is bounded to the east by the islands of the Lesser Antilles, to the north by the Greater Antilles and to the west and south by the mainland of Central and South America. In area it totals about 2.5 million square kilometres (1 million square miles). In distance, the furthest extent (Trinidad to the eastern end of Cuba) is about 2800 km (1750 miles), which is roughly the distance from Chicago to San Francisco and more than that from London to Istanbul.

To the north and west is the Gulf of Mexico. It receives sea water via the narrow Yucatan Channel between Mexico and Cuba. This water has already passed through the Caribbean so is somewhat different from the pristine ocean water that enters into that sea in westerly flowing currents from the Atlantic. The coast of the Gulf of Mexico is mainly the seaboards of Mexico and southern United States, from which many major rivers discharge their sediment-laden fresh water. These factors, together with a more northerly location, create a body of water with its own individual characteristics distinctly different from the Caribbean.

Outside the Caribbean to the north and east lies the Great Bahamas Bank, a large area of shallow sea much of which is north of the Tropic of Cancer. In this direction the Florida Peninsula stretches towards the Caribbean. On its west coast are the shallow Florida Banks and the Gulf of Mexico while to the east is the Atlantic coast bathed in water most of which is pouring out of the Gulf between Florida and Cuba. This current together with some Atlantic water runs north and east to become the Gulf Stream. Thus for various reasons the marine biology of the Gulf, the Florida coasts and (to a lesser extent) the Bahamas differs from the Caribbean. None the less there are considerable similarities and much of this book will be applicable to shores from the southern United States to Venezuela.

Fig 1.4 *The Caribbean, especially the eastern region, is still volcanically active and subject to occasional earthquakes. This photograph was taken in Montserrat on 1 August 1997.*

The geological history of the Caribbean region explains the distribution of the islands and dictates the nature of the rocky and sandy shores. More will be said about the latter in the chapters devoted to them but it is worth while to review briefly some of the major features. Most of the Caribbean Sea lies above a section of ocean floor called the Caribbean Plate. This whole section of seabed is moving westwards at about 2 cm (0.8 in) per year. At its western end this plate is in collision with the Cocos Plate which is moving eastwards at about three times that speed. This collision is the reason for the volcanic and earthquake activity in much of central Mexico. The eastern (Atlantic) edge of the Caribbean Plate is also subject to collision, this time by the westward moving North and South American Plates which have higher rates of movement. As a result the American plates are thrust downwards under the Caribbean Plate which in turn results in considerable volcanic activity just to the west of this line of subduction. Over time these volcanoes have thrown up a chain of islands which now form the Lesser Antilles running from Grenada in the south to Anguilla in the north. This volcanic activity continues today with recent eruptions in St Vincent (1902, 1974), Martinique (1902) Guadeloupe (1903, 1956, 1977) and most recently in Montserrat (1995–7). Montserrat's Soufrière Hills Volcano has spewed out ash, rocks and gases to such an extent that now (2004) 65% of the island is uninhabitable; only in the northern third have islanders returned. Tourism is gradually being restored to this lovely island but at the time of writing access is only by ferry or helicopter due to the destruction of the airport on 25 June 1997 (when 8 million cubic metres of the volcano's dome avalanched in 20 minutes).

The islands of the Greater Antilles (Cuba to Puerto Rico) are older. Except for Cuba, they lie roughly on the junction of the northern edge of the Caribbean Plate where it borders the North American Plate. At this point the two plates are moving in the same direction so presently volcanic activity does not occur. However as the North American Plate is moving at a faster rate the sliding movement between the plates does produce some earthquakes (Puerto Rico, 1918; Dominican Republic, 1946; Jamaica, 1907). These islands, being older, have a more complex geology. Although volcanic rocks are still in evidence they have often be overlain by sedimentary rocks.

Tides, winds and exposure

Tides

Most seashores around the world are subjected to tides whereby the water level rises and falls, usually about twice per day. The major reason for these tides is the gravitational attraction of the moon. The part of the ocean nearest to the moon is drawn towards it, creating a bulge in the sea surface. On the side of the earth away from the moon, the moon's gravitational force acts more strongly on the Earth than on the sea which is 'left behind' to

create a second watery bulge. As the earth turns in its daily revolution any point on the oceans or at the shore experiences these two bulges as high tides with corresponding low tides between. The usual tidal cycle is 12.5 hours, thus each day the tides progress by an hour. So if high tide is 10.00 am today you would expect another at 10.30 pm and again next day at 11.00 am; you might also predict low tides at about 4.15 pm and 4.45 am.

Fig 1.5 *Many of the Caribbean islands have rocks composed of fossilised coral reefs. Closer examination usually reveals not only corals but also a range of fossil molluscs and other invertebrates.*

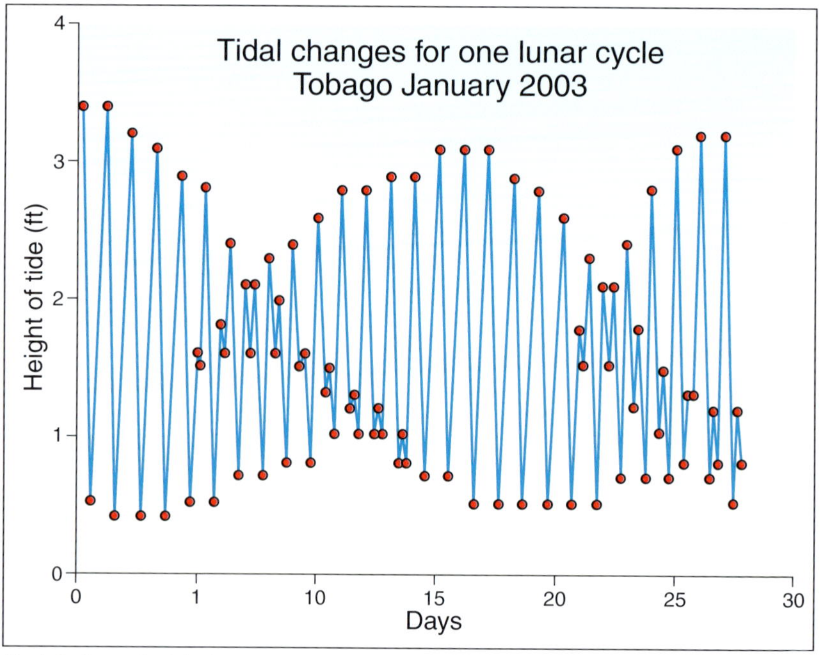

Fig 1.6 *A graph of the high and low tides during a lunar cycle for Tobago. See text for details.*

This programme of tides is further complicated by the gravitational attraction of the sun, which although much further away than the moon is much greater in mass and therefore influential in the tidal rhythm. When the sun and the moon are aligned (at new and full moon) the two forces are added producing larger, so-called spring, tides, with higher 'highs' and lower 'lows'. At first and third quarters of the moon the influences of the sun and moon are at right angles and so reduce tides to minimum, or neap, tides. In temperate regions there is also a seasonal tidal rhythm with the biggest spring tides occurring around the time of the equinoxes (March and September).

In some places these tides may be very large. The world's largest tides occur in the Minas Basin, part of the Bay of Fundy in Nova Scotia. Here the difference in sea level between high and low tides (tidal range) may reach 16 m (52 ft). Tides of about 10 m (32 ft) are found in a number of places in Europe, North America and Australia but values of 3–5 m (10–16 ft) are more typical.

In the Caribbean tides are generally regarded as small although there is considerable variation within the region. Furthermore they often exhibit a different rhythm from that seen in temperate regions and described above. Figure 1.6 shows the tidal rhythm for Tobago for the duration of one lunar cycle. True to the typical expectation, the spring and neap tides can be clearly seen. Also, as already mentioned, the tidal range is small compared with most of Europe and North America, being less than a metre at springs and only about half that at neaps. The biggest difference from the typical pattern seen in temperate regions is in the frequency of tides. As already explained, the 'normal' situation is to have two highs and two lows each day (or more accurately about 25 hours). As can be seen in Fig 1.6, Tobago experiences (as does much of the Caribbean) only one high and one low each day for about half of the lunar month and two of each for the other half. However, even when there are two highs and two lows per day they are of very unequal size with the smaller really having very little influence on the inhabitants of the shore. This has a real significance for beachcombers who may be used to European or North American tidal regimes. You may observe a morning low tide and expect to go collecting again that evening only to find that this coincides with high tide! First experience of this is bewildering and confusing for the unwary.

Tides are one of the factors that make seashores so different from, say, lakeshores. The seashore is not simply a sharp boundary between land and water; the exact position of that demarcation moves up and down inexorably each day. Thus between the high and low tide marks is an area which is neither land nor sea but sometimes one and sometimes the other. This intertidal zone is the subject of much of this book. Seaweeds and animals living here must be adapted to spending at least some of their time in both the aquatic and the terrestrial world. Of course, as we have seen above, the lowest of low tides only occur a few times per year so that creatures exposed by these need only survive out of water for a very short time and only infrequently. Similarly those at the top of the beach may only be inundated on rare occasions. However for most beach animals and seaweeds the norm will be an alternation between being in or out of the sea once or twice each day. Much of the fascination of these organisms lies in the many and wonderful ways in which they have become adapted to cope with this constantly shifting set of demands. Obviously creatures living near the top of the intertidal area will be covered for less time than those living near the low tide mark. Because different species have different tolerances to immersion there will be a change in the nature of the living community as one moves up the shore. For convenience this can be divided into a number of zones. This phenomenon of zonation is best seen on rocky shores and so will be dealt with in more detail in Chapter 3.

The extent of the intertidal zone will depend on two factors: the vertical distance between the water levels at high and low tide, and the slope of the beach. Thus a large tidal range over a gently sloping sandy beach will lay bare a huge area of sand at each low tide. On the other hand a small tidal range at a vertical rock face will expose a very narrow band each tide. We have already seen that Caribbean tides are fairly small in range, especially compared with Europe and North America, so visitors from these regions should not expect to see beaches exposed to the same extent as at home. It is also true to say that gently sloping sandy beaches are probably less a feature of the Caribbean than of temperate regions so those expecting the sea to retreat to the horizon at low tide will be disappointed. (They should try Blackpool or Morecambe!) Indeed one has to say that in many parts of the Caribbean the tides may be hardly detectable.

Winds

The Caribbean is famous for its trade winds which blow predominantly from the northeast. These are a refreshing feature of life for much of the year throughout the region. For shore life they mean that east-facing coasts are likely to be subject to the action of wind-generated waves. In contrast, west-facing shores are often sheltered from these waves and have calm beaches. The classic examples are the east and west coasts of Barbados although similar situations exist in many places. Because of the constant nature of the trade winds the wave action on any particular beach is fairly constant year round. However, this predictable situation can be disturbed during the late summer and autumn (hurricane season) by the appearance of storms which vary from short spells of heavy rain and squally winds right through to full hurricanes with winds in excess of 118 kmph (74 mph) and torrential rainfall.

In most years there will be a few such hurricanes but often they are mild and damage is limited. None the less, on occasions their violence can be awe inspiring and astonishingly profound. In September 2004 Hurricane Ivan, the most powerful hurricane for a decade, swept through the region striking the southern islands of the Lesser Antilles and then passing over the Cayman Islands, Jamaica, Cuba, Mexico and the southern states of the United States leaving a trail of death and destruction. Grenada fared worst with 220 kmph (140 mph) winds damaging or destroying 90% of homes and leaving 39 dead. Needless to say, such violent weather has a devastating effect on inshore

Fig 1.7 *Hurricanes occur regularly in late summer although any one island will usually experience these intense storms relatively infrequently. However, when they strike the effects can be extremely damaging (as in Grenada and other places with Hurricane Ivan in 2004). As well as wreaking havoc on land, hurricanes can destroy shores and beaches as well as affecting beachside vegetation.*

marine habitats. Coral reefs are smashed, seagrass beds churned up, mangrove trees felled and sand beaches washed away leaving degraded conditions for plant and animal life. Some regeneration will take place rapidly but many of the effects will be long lasting or even permanent.

Exposure and the effects of waves

Shores which are prone to a constant level of wave action are said to be subjected to a certain level of **exposure**. Thus the sheltered shores of an enclosed bay with very small waves or no waves are relatively unexposed while rocky cliffs open to the full force of ocean swells will be rated as highly exposed. The animals and plants of these differently exposed beaches will be characteristic. One obvious feature of exposed shores is that the

Fig 1.8 *Beaches may be more or less exposed to wind and wave action. This is Trellis Bay, Tortola, which rates very low on the exposure scale. It is sheltered from the prevailing winds by its deep crescent shape, which faces north, and the presence of offshore islands.*

Fig 1.9 *The open east coast of Barbados is constantly pounded by ocean breakers driven on the easterly trade winds that have blown across the full width of the Atlantic Ocean. In storm conditions this beach is extremely exposed.*

inhabitants must either be attached to the substrate or at least able to attach themselves firmly to avoid being washed away. On less exposed shores more delicate and mobile forms can survive. Often on rocky shores it is possible to grade exposure on the basis of the animals and plants that are present.

Another way in which waves affect shore creatures is by the surge and splash that they create. In the absence of waves, the shore immediately above the high tide mark will remain dry. With wave action there may be complete soaking for some distance above the 'still water' high tide mark and splashing even higher, perhaps for many metres. This effectively extends the width of the shore that marine animals and plants can inhabit.

The downside of wave action is, of course, the habitat damage that is caused in extreme cases, especially that occurring during hurricanes and tropical storms. After such storms beaches may be much altered (see Fig 7.10). Sand may have been removed or shifted, rocks might have been fragmented or rolled over and mangrove trees can be broken or even uprooted. The effects on the animals and plants living in these places can be profound and long lasting, and in some cases permanent. The damage to offshore, underwater coral reefs, although devastating, might seem outside the scope of this book. Not so. If coral reefs are broken or destroyed (as they can be by heavy wave action), the effects on the intertidal zone can be many and varied. Most importantly the reef often acts as a buffer against normal wave action, with waves partially breaking and losing energy before they reach the shoreline. Without the reef these waves may now break directly on the shore. As a result animals and plants previously used to sheltered conditions may perish, rocky shores may experience new, more vigorous erosion and sandy shores may have their sand removed. Similar changes may occur if reefs are removed by man's agency as sometimes happens when explosives are used. Often this action is carried out in the misguided belief that the removal of coral will produce a better sandy beach for tourists. The result is usually the opposite to that expected and beaches may disappear completely.

Characteristics of sea water and the influence of fresh water

The Caribbean Sea is warm (one of the many reasons why we all love it so). Temperatures are typically in the high 20s Celsius. On the west coast of Barbados the annual range is from 26 to 29.6°C and for the north coast of Jamaica the values are 27.9 to 28.7°C with shallow bays being perhaps half a degree warmer. These figures illustrate not only how warm the water is but also how relatively constant the temperature is; compare them with typical annual ranges for the English Channel of 9 to 16°C and the west coast of Scotland of 5 to 16°C. These constant high temperatures ensure that, other conditions being favourable, growth and reproduction continue apace. As most of the animals on seashores are cold blooded, the warm sea water also results in their being able to move very much faster than their temperate equivalents. As a result starfish seem almost to gallop and crabs are lightning fast. Life is lived at a faster tempo. It is worth while mentioning here that many seashore animals and plants spend much of their time out of the water and during the day the heat generated by the sun can become too much of a good thing (as it may for many visitors). It is hard to believe how many invertebrates that cling to rocks, such as limpets and mussels, can survive the searing midday sun.

Sea water is salty and one feature of the open ocean is that the **salinity** (saltiness) is relatively constant at about 36.5 practical salinity units (psu). The Caribbean is often slightly less saline than that, for example at Puerto Rico it varies from 36.1 to 34.2 psu over the course of a year. The lowest values occur in the latter part of the year and are attributed in equal parts to the rainfall that occurs at that time and to the outflow from the Orinoco River which discharges into the Atlantic just south of Trinidad. Interestingly, the peak outflow from the Orinoco occurs in mid-summer and it appears that this riverine water takes about three months to reach the northeastern Caribbean. Pools of relatively dilute sea water (about 34.5 psu) have been detected off the coast of Barbados too and these are attributed to the influence of fresh water from the Amazon. However, these small variations in salinity are unlikely to have much effect on shore life. Indeed, many inshore environments are subject to occasional or constant dilution by rain, rivers or groundwater. This is especially true for mangrove swamps.

Outflow from rivers not only brings fresh water but often also carries suspended silt. As many shore animals feed by filtering sea water there is always the chance that this silt will clog their delicate sieving mechanisms. Other hazards that can be brought down by rivers include a variety of chemicals (mainly of agricultural or industrial origin) and organic wastes, which can lead to changes in the seashore environment. These pollution issues will be discussed in Chapter 7.

Fig 1.10 *These barnacle shells show two interesting features: firstly, there are two species present, the smaller growing on the larger; secondly, the permanent nature of barnacle settlement is illustrated by the upturned piece, lower right, which has clearly been scraped off the hull of a fishing boat. The barnacles were so firmly fixed that the paint came off with them.*

What sorts of things do we find on shore?

Living inhabitants

On rocky shores and in mangrove swamps living animals and plants are usually present and obvious, often in considerable numbers. Sandy shores offer fewer examples of live creatures that can be seen without a search. Most easily observed are the **sessile** or **attached** organisms. These are attached to the substrate on which they live, such as a rock or a mangrove root. They may be fixed for life (sessile), unable to survive or reattach if removed, such as barnacles or sponges. Alternatively, they may be firmly adherent for much of the time but able to move about, usually when covered at high tide or during darkness (attached). These latter include limpets and chitons. Some of these animals cling on much more firmly than others; limpets are very difficult to detach but snails such as the nerites can be removed fairly easily. Sessile and attached animals are lacking from sandy beaches because of the shifting nature of the substrate. Other shore inhabitants may be fully mobile, the obvious examples being a wide range of crabs.

Seaweeds and lichens are also to be found attached to hard structures on the beach. There are various types to be found in different zones up the beach.

Although some beach dwellers are easy to see, many others hide away from view. On rocky shores this may be under stones or in crevices and under ledges. Keeping out of sight may have to do with avoiding predators or it may be to avoid the heating and drying effects of the tropical sun. Many such animals come out after dark or when submerged by sea water. On sandy beaches many animals are buried in the substrate and either live out their lives digging through it or perhaps communicating with the surface via an open burrow. Beneath the relatively featureless surface there may be a rich and complex world.

Live (or recently dead) animals and plants from elsewhere

The tides and waves will wash up organisms which do not live normally in the place where you find them. A classic example is the Portuguese man-of-war, a relative of the jellyfish, which floats at the surface of tropical oceans, trailing its tentacles down into the sea. It floats by virtue of a gas-filled bladder and has no control over its movement being completely controlled by the wind. Due to the prevailing northeasterly trade winds many of these striking animals are stranded on east-facing Caribbean beaches. Storm conditions often lead to other offshore animals being washed up on beaches. The most vulnerable are those with limited control over their movements such as sea urchins and bivalve molluscs. You may also find dead or dying birds and fish. Some of the latter may be discarded catch or bait from fishermen so don't assume some sort of ecological incident on the basis of a few such cases. There are also those animals that are really sea dwellers but

Fig 1.11 *Some species of* Sargassum *weed spend their whole life cycle afloat but others live attached to rocks and coral. Both types are commonly washed up on to shores.*

which invade the shore when the tide comes up and are sometimes stranded as the sea retreats. This can happen with some fish and crustaceans.

Seaweeds are also frequently detached from sublittoral (below low tide) locations and finish washed up on the shore. The genus of brown seaweed, *Sargassum*, contains many attached species and two species that are never attached and complete their whole life cycle floating.

Parts of dead animals and plants

These constitute much of what the beachcomber finds when patrolling the strandline. Most obviously sought after are shells. These are usually either from snails or bivalves and may be in a wide range of conditions from pristine to badly eroded. Shells which have been washed around in surf, abraided by sand and stones are quickly damaged and, of course, are finally ground down to tiny pieces which will become components of the sand itself; indeed some beaches are made almost entirely from shell fragments. Apart from the usually obvious molluscan remains, many other animal groups will be present in this category in particular those of crustacea. Crustaceans are animals whose bodies are encased in a jointed skeleton.

Fig 1.12 *Shells are the most frequently found, and often the most prized, objects for beachcombers. Caribbean shores offer rich and varied opportunities.*

Typical examples are crabs and lobsters. Most echinoderms have hard parts too, usually composed of spines and plates. The globular tests (shells) of sea urchins are frequent finds on many Caribbean shores. Fragments of coral are also commonly found and indeed some beaches are almost wholly made up of coral, either quite large pieces or perhaps ground into the startlingly white sand so characteristic of some islands. Many other groups of animals have hard parts that turn up occasionally and these will be dealt with in the appropriate chapters.

The most obvious dead plants to be washed up are the various algae, which have calcareous skeletons such as *Halimeda* and *Amphiroa*. In life these seaweeds are coloured to a greater or lesser extent by the pigments in the living tissues. After death only the limy, pure white skeleton remains. These too will be ground into sand grains.

Fig 1.13 *Crustaceans have jointed skeletons that fragment easily after death. Detached limbs and claws are common finds on the shore but are often quite difficult to identify. They have their own aesthetic appeal and make delightful subjects for sketches. Drawing and painting shore material is a good way to sharpen one's observational skills as well as a means of producing evocative holiday souvenirs.*

Objects of land origin

On beaches one often finds seeds and fruits which have originated from land plants. Their most usual routes to the beach are either via runoff from the land (streams or rivers) or by being shed directly into the sea by overhanging trees and bushes. Many seeds can survive immersion in sea water and the sea is a major distributor for some tree species including the coconut palm. Heavy rain will also wash land snail shells down gullies and streams into the sea. These may then reappear on beaches and be very confusing for the shell collector.

Fig 1.14 *These white, limy objects are the skeletons of calcareous seaweeds. They fragment easily after death and are major contributors of grains to white sand beaches. On the right are two examples of the green alga,* Halimeda, *while on the left are two specimens of calcareous red algae, probably from the genus* Amphiroa.

Box 1.1 Filter feeding

Sea water contains many small particles. These may be living creatures, microscopic algae or planktonic animals, or they may be suspended pieces of detritus derived from organic material. This material may originate from dead animal or plant parts which have been broken down by biological or physical means into small fragments or they may be of faecal origin. The particles often have large numbers of bacteria on or in them and can constitute a rich food resource. As a result many marine animals have evolved to exploit them by means of fine filters. These animals are called filter (or suspension) feeders.

There are two main types of filter feeders: (i) those that are passive and rely on existing water currents to bring the particles to their filters; and (ii) those that are active and create currents which they then filter. Examples of the former include some brittle stars which lift up one or more of their arms into the water (while holding on to the substrate with the others) and catch particles on sticky tube feet on their arms. This food is then passed to the mouth. Many of the fanworms, which have an inverted cone of colourful tentacles, use similar passive means of filtering.

Active filter feeders employ many means of creating currents. Probably the commonest seashore examples are the bivalve molluscs. Inside the shells is a space, the mantle cavity, which communicates with the sea through two tubes (siphons). Water is drawn in through one siphon and is passed through gills, which have a fine sieve-like structure. Suspended particles are caught here and passed to the mouth while the sea water exits from the mantle cavity via the second siphon. The driving force for the current passing through the gills is tiny hair-like structures (cilia) which beat in a coordinated way to move the water. Sponges use similar means to pull in water through very many tiny holes in their surface. After being sieved the water exits from one or more larger holes. Skeletons of dead sponges found on the beach often show where these exit pores would have been.

Filter feeding animals are particularly susceptible to fouling by either excessive amounts of organic particles or heavy suspensions of fine sand or mud particles. Both of these can overload or clog their filters, sometimes resulting in death.

2 Sandy Shores

The classic concept of beachcombing is that of collecting shells on the strandline of a golden sandy shore. What we hope to do in this chapter is to explain the nature of such a shore; how and why it is the way it is, and to help you to identify the things you find. Shells of course will be a major part of your finds but it is probable that other groups will be represented. Seaweeds will also occur and we must not forget that these beaches are the places where turtles come ashore to lay their eggs. In addition many birds feed along the sea's edge or in the shallows just offshore but we will deal with these in Chapter 6.

What is sand?

Obviously sand is composed of individual grains. These may vary in size and also in their origin. According to the Wentworth scale sand grains range in size from 2 mm ('very coarse sand') through five grades to 'very fine sand' having a size as small as 62 µm (1 µm is one thousandth of a millimetre, about one twenty-five thousandth of an inch). Below that size the particles are considered as silt and are typical of mud. Particles larger than 2 mm

Fig 2.1 *A sample of fairly coarse sand magnified to show the nature of the grains. Note that some of them are fragments of bivalve and gastropod shells, echinoderm spines and small pieces of coral.*

(about a twelfth of an inch) are graded as pebbles or cobbles. On any given beach sand grains will vary in size but often one particular size grade dominates so that it is relatively easy to identify coarse or fine sand by feel or appearance. There is also an obvious correlation between the coarseness of the sand and the size of the waves; the finest sands occur where waves are small while surf-pounded beaches have large-grained sand or may even be of shingle or pebbles. This is because the waves wash away the smaller grains and the bigger the waves the larger the grains they can remove. We also see that coarse-sand beaches are steeper than fine-sand ones.

Sand grains are made from a range of materials. They may come from erosive activity on local rocks. Thus some islands in the Caribbean have black beaches as a result of the breakdown of the local volcanic rocks. In some of the older islands quartz grains may dominate, again derived from local rocks. Many of the famous white beaches of the region are from fragmented coral, either from offshore reefs or from the fossil reefs in nearby rocks. It is claimed that parrotfish are significant producers of coral fragments which result when they crush the surface of coral heads to eat the living tissue. The coral skeleton is ingested but passes through the gut and reappears in the faeces. One estimate suggests that a natural population of stoplight parrotfish can produce more than 2 tonnes of sediment per hectare per year in this way. Seaweeds with limy skeletons, such as *Padina*, may also contribute significantly to beach sand. Much sand is produced in the sea but some is the result of terrestrial weathering with the particles entering the sea from streams and rivers. Various animal-derived materials other than coral are encountered in sand. Shells of molluscs can be an important component with additional contributions from echinoderm shells and spines as well as from crab and lobster shells.

Life in sand

When one looks at a sandy shore signs of life are usually absent (except for birds and tourists). This contrasts with rocky shores where living plants and animals usually abound. The reason for the difference is mainly because sand dwellers live in, rather than on, their substrate; they are buried and thus out of sight. The shifting, unstable nature of sand enforces this difference and it contrasts with mud too in that permanent burrows can be maintained in this latter, firmer material. However sand offers advantages for its inhabitants. Being hidden below the surface affords considerable protection from predation while the relatively slow water movement through sand buffers those in it against short-term changes in temperature and salinity. In temperate climates, which often have a larger tidal range than the Caribbean (see Fig 1.6), vast areas of sand may be uncovered at each low tide. In the Caribbean this is not usually the case so intertidal sand-dwelling animals are relatively few; most sand creatures live sublittorally (below the low tide mark) and come to the beachcomber's attention when they are washed up.

Fine sand with its small grains is relatively firm and along with the associated small waves may permit the creation of permanent burrows. One such sand dweller is the mantis shrimp, which lives in a burrow that may be U-shaped or have more than two openings. The shrimp itself has one pair of legs adapted for slashing and stabbing and so fast are the movement of these appendages that they can dismember other small crustaceans which often are its prey. Sometimes it will sit in the mouth of its burrow to ambush passers-by but especially at night it will venture forth to hunt in the open. Occasionally they are washed up on beaches. Do not touch unless you are sure it is dead as its nickname of 'thumb splitter' is well deserved. Some species of burrowing animal may reinforce their burrow with a tube of their own manufacture. Many species of marine worm do this and sometimes the tops of their tubes can be seen at the water's edge at low tide.

Coarser sand and the associated greater wave action militate against permanent burrows but make it easier for animals to move about inside the sand. Such animals include the two-spined starfish, which moves about below the surface of the substrate searching for its bivalve mollusc food. Dead or dying specimens are washed up occasionally. Some sea urchins also live in sand, including the reef echinoneus and the sand dollar and its relatives. Predatory snails such as natica and the moon shells plough through sand in search of bivalve prey. In life they extend much of their body out of the shell which becomes almost enclosed in soft flesh. Presumably this is to protect the shell against abrasion from the sand. It is certainly the case that dead specimens of these shells when washed up are frequently in superb condition, often better than the shells of live snails living on rocks such as the Caribbean top shell.

Fig 2.2 *The mantis shrimp lives in a U-shaped burrow in sand and is sometimes washed up on beaches. It can deliver a fierce slash with its claws so do not pick it up unless you are sure it is dead.*

Types of sandy shore

As already indicated, sandy shores may have large or small waves accompanied by a steeper or shallower slope and larger or smaller average grain size. These factors will affect the typical flora and fauna of the intertidal and sublittoral zones and thus what appears for the beachcomber. By and large the geological origin of the sand will have much less effect on the biota. However, the nature of the sublittoral habitat just offshore will be very influential in what turns up on the strandline. Thus if a wave-swept beach has more sand offshore expect to find a considerable number of bivalves, such as donax, capable of living in this shifting substrate and burrowing predators like the snail natica. If the nearby seabed is rocky then many of the things that turn up will have been attached forms such as arc shells, mussels and sea fans. In the Caribbean many sandy shores have coral reefs offshore which yield many of the attached forms found on rocks but also some items specific to such reefs including pieces of the coral itself. In calm bays seagrass will grow in the shallow water giving the seabed a dark appearance from a distance. There are a number of different species of

Fig 2.3 *The cushion star is common in seagrass beds and may appear either on the beach or in very shallow water in quiet sandy bays. Sadly they have been over-collected in some areas to sell as tourist souvenirs.*

seagrass, all of them classified as flowering plants (although some have never been known to flower). The commonest is turtle grass which has strap-shaped leaves 4–12 mm ($\frac{1}{8}$ – $\frac{1}{2}$ in) wide having 9–15 parallel veins. They can only grow in relatively quiet and stable conditions but once established the seagrasses further consolidate the sand because of their spreading, rhizomatous root systems. This stability encourages a rich flora and fauna to develop while above the substrate the mini-forest of fronds is an environment full of fish and invertebrates. Grass beds are important nursery beds for some young animals which, when larger, will move to live in deeper water. For example, the queen conch and the spiny lobster, both commercially important species, often spend their early lives here.

What you might find on a sandy shore

Sponges

These animals are attached in life, living on rock and other hard substrates or even on living things such as seagrass. While some species have a fairly well defined shape, many others are more amorphous simply moulding themselves to the underlying surface. They are soft bodied, supported by a skeleton of protein fibres, and, in some cases, silica spicules. Although recently detached specimens may occur washed up on beaches, it is more usual to find the proteinaceous skeletons. Sponges are filter feeders and even in the skeletons it is often possible to see the position of the large oscula which are the exit pores for the filtered water. Because many species lack a fixed form, naming of washed-up skeletons is difficult. However, both the vase sponge and tube sponges have sufficiently consistent shapes to permit their identification.

Anthozoa (gorgonians, anemones and corals)

This group is hugely important in tropical shallow waters. Not only do the corals build the reefs which are so characteristic of the region but the gorgonians form submarine forests of sea feathers, whips and fans. The sea anemones are perhaps a somewhat less important group in the tropics compared with temperate seas but none the less they are a major component of the shallow water ecosystem. The basic anthozoan body plan is a cylindrical creature bearing one or more rings of tentacles at the upper end. In the centre of these tentacles is a mouth, the entrance and exit for the sac-shaped gut. Anemones are usually solitary and live with the base of the body attached to some hard object although some live with most of the body buried in sand and only the tentacles visible. The other two groups live in large colonies derived from a single organism. Each individual of the colony is called a polyp and looks rather like a small anemone. The colony produces a hard external skeleton into which the polyps can withdraw. Anthozoans are

Fig 2.4 *This sponge skeleton still retains the shape of the living animal. The two large holes are the oscula – channels through which the feeding current exits the sponge.*

mainly filter feeders, which rely on small animals blundering into their tentacles that are armed with stinging cells. For creatures that feed this way the advantages of a skeleton that can raise the colony high into the water are obvious. For beachcombers the most usual finds are these skeletal materials. Corals manufacture a stony (calcium carbonate) skeleton while that of gorgonians is of a hard but flexible protein surrounded by a layer of tissue that may contain calcium carbonate.

Many whole or fragmented gorgonians can be found washed up on sandy shores especially those with rock or coral offshore. The easiest to identify are probably the sea fans. The **common sea fan** has its branches compressed in the plane of the fan while those of the **Bahamian sea fan** are compressed at right angles to the plane of the fan. Sea plumes are also frequently found and there are a number of common species although they are usually difficult to differentiate in tideline collections. The polyps of gorgonians are small but close examination of the skeletons should reveal the tiny pits in which they lived.

Fig 2.5 *Many sandy shores that have nearby reefs will be littered with fragments of coral skeleton. The white sand against which these were photographed may be largely composed of finely ground coral. The two specimens in the lower right clearly show the positions that the coral polyps had occupied. These marks are smaller in the central branch of* Acropora *while in the brain coral (top left) the polyps have extended to form linear markings.*

Coral fragments will be found, sometimes in huge abundance, where there are reefs offshore. Coral polyps are often larger than those of gorgonians and in some species their original locations on the skeleton are easy to see, for example in *Oculina*. In other forms the polyps may be relatively small and closely packed (for example in the *Acropora* species and **starlet coral**). As the coral grows the polyps divide to form new ones but in some species this division is incomplete so that what is produced is a folded, linear effect typically seen in the brain corals. In worn fragments of coral the original siting of the polyps may be difficult to see but often these polished pieces have a beauty of their own.

Anemones are more usually found on rocky shores and, as they do not have a hard skeleton, no trace of them is usually seen on the tideline. However, at low tide you may see the disc and tentacle rings of buried anemones. There are two or three sand-dwelling species found in our region. The **brown striped sand anemone** has tiny wart-like tentacles and the upper surfaces appear to have seven radial bands of brown colouring on a paler background. The **collared sea anemone** has an olive or brown disc on which are many radiating grooves.

The group **Hydrozoa** contains relatives of the anthozoans and in many cases they have polyps similar to those of corals. In the case of **fire corals**

Fig 2.6 *Sea fans are frequent finds on the strandline. In life the meshwork of the fan is covered with living tissue and a host of tiny hydra-like polyps. These feed on plankton that wash up against the fan.*

there is a calcium carbonate skeleton, but unlike the true corals the polyps are so tiny that their positions on the skeleton are only visible as tiny pinprick holes. Thus the appearance is smoother than for true corals and fresh specimens are honey-coloured. Fire corals live in shallow water and sometimes protrude above the surface at low tide. Do not handle live fire corals as their stinging cells can deliver a strong burning sensation which persists for some time. Dead and often eroded fragments of skeleton commonly appear on beaches with reefs offshore.

Another hydrozoan that is frequently encountered on sandy beaches also stings, more venomously than fire coral. This villain is the **Portuguese man-of-war**. What one sees at first, washed up on the strandline, is a brilliantly coloured, violet balloon-like object anything up to 15 cm (6 in) long. On closer examination it is usually possible to see a mass of dark purple tentacles attached to the undersurface. This animal spends its life drifting in the ocean with the gas-filled float at the surface and the tentacles, which are capable of great extension, hanging down into the sea to depths of 18 m (60 ft). These tentacles carry stinging cells which can paralyse fish and other prey.

Fig 2.7 *The beauty of the Portuguese man-of-war belies its ability to deliver a debilitating sting. Normally this creature floats at the surface of the open ocean with its tentacles extending for metres down into water where they ensnare and paralyse their prey such as fish. At the mercy of the wind, they are often stranded on beaches in large numbers. The tentacles of even seemingly dead specimens can sting and should be avoided.*

Fig 2.8 *Mason worms live just at the edge of the sea on calm sandy beaches. They make tubes of sand grains and other material into which they can retreat if danger threatens. These tubes have been dug up, but in life they can be easily located as the top few millemetres protrude above the surface.*

Although the Portuguese man-of-war appears to be a single organism, it is in fact a colony of many individuals where there is considerable specialisation between the members so that some polyps bear the stinging cells while others are responsible for digestion, reproduction and so on. It is best not to handle this animal even after it has been stranded. The stings from the tentacles, even detached pieces, can be severe enough to require immediate medical attention and minor contacts alone can be extremely painful. If you see the floats in the sea do not swim nearby as touching the extended tentacles may produce lines of stings looking like a whiplash. A less venomous relative is the so-called **By-the-wind sailor**. The float in this animal is much less inflated but carries a sail set at an angle to its long axis. Sometimes these creatures are blown on to beaches in great numbers.

Annelid worms are less well represented on Caribbean beaches than in temperate regions, but in quiet bays one often sees the tops of worm tubes protruding from fine sand or mud. These tubes are constructed from pieces of shell, seagrass leaves or other debris and held together by a leathery material secreted by the worm inside and which gives it the name of **shaggy parchment tubeworm**. Although the tubes are fairly obvious the worm is more difficult to see unless the whole length of the tube is excavated, an action which will certainly lead to the eventual death of the worm and probably destroy a few of its neighbours too. Other tube-dwelling worms that are sometimes visible in just a few centimetres of water are the **fanworms**. These have a circle of head tentacles arranged in an inverted cone which acts as a filter to remove food from the water that passes by.

Fig 2.9 *Ghost crabs are common on many sandy shores. They are often seen, like the one shown here, near their burrows but will venture further from home in search of food.*

Arthropods are animals with a jointed skeleton on the outside of their bodies. The group includes insects, spiders and scorpions but most of the marine and shore-dwelling arthropods are **Crustacea**. (The main features of this group can be found in Box 3.2 on page 87.) Under this heading come obvious candidates such as crabs and lobsters but also some lesser known animals like the hoppers and slaters as well as a host of planktonic animals. The commonest examples on sandy shores are the **ghost crabs**. These live in burrows either within the wave-swept zone or just above the high tide mark. From a distance these pale crabs will often be seen 'ghosting' across the sand surface in search of food. But approach too close and they will flee down their burrows in an instant. If you sit close by, your patience may be rewarded by their eventual reappearance – but don't bank on it. The entrances to their burrows are often damaged by waves or passing pedestrians and with luck you may be able to see the repair process going on. The crab will retreat into the hole and then periodically appear pushing a pile of sand with its claws; at the entrance this will be thrown some distance by a vigorous jerk of one claw. A number of other crabs live in the sand just below the low tide mark in water of about a metre deep. These can be glimpsed in shallow water sometimes and their bodies appear washed up occasionally. Examples include the two species of box crabs. These live buried in sandy seabeds and are also known as the shamefaced crabs as the claws, which are wide and flat, are held close together covering the animal's 'face'. The claws are powerful and used to

Fig 2.10 *This is the claw of the common box crab. The knob at the base of the movable part of the claw is used like a tin opener to enable the crab to feed on gastropod molluscs. The wide frilled basal section of the claw is used to protect the 'face' of the crab when it lies hidden, buried in the sand.*

crack open mollusc prey. The smaller species (**common box crab**) is typically less than 5 cm (2 in) across the carapace and is a pale sandy colour. The larger (8–10 cm, $3\frac{1}{2}$–4 in) **flame box crab** is less often seen in tideline debris but is easily distinguished by its greyish carapace streaked with flame-shaped areas of reddish brown. Another crab whose skeleton is frequently found on the strandline is the **blue crab**. This and its relatives have very wide carapaces with elongated spines at the widest part. In life they inhabit shallow water over sandy or muddy seabeds.

The external armour of lobsters can also to be found on the beach. The **spiny lobster** is fairly common in the Caribbean although large specimens are rare in most places due to overfishing. This species is different from the lobster, which usually appears on tables in the eastern United States and northern Europe, in that it lacks large claws. The skeletons are usually bluish in colour but may be green or brown.

A whole range of small crustaceans live in the drying seaweed and seagrass rubbish that washes up on beaches. Mostly they belong to two subgroups that are different from the crabs and lobsters, namely the isopods and the amphipods. If you plunge tideline vegetation into sea water these creatures will often swim out and be spotted. Usually they are about 1 cm (0.4 in) or so in length and elongate. Amphipods tend to swim on their sides

Fig 2.11 *This is the carapace (back of the body) of the larger flamed box crab. The front of the animal would have been at the top of the picture.*

and when out of water they can often jump. Isopods look like the European woodlouse to which they are related. Worldwide these two groups boast over 15 000 species but their identification tends to be specialist territory.

Molluscs are usually represented on sandy beaches by the dead shell remains which are washed ashore. It is these that most often attract attention from beachcombers and many happy hours can be spent strolling along the strandline, head down, searching for that illusive perfect specimen. 'Just a few more metres', you think, only to find eventually that the pockets are bursting and that the pre-dinner drink has been almost missed.

There are two major types of mollusc to be considered here, the gastropods and the bivalves (more properly members of the classes Gastropoda and Pelecypoda respectively). The main features of these two groups are shown in Boxes 2.1 and 2.2 on page 50.

Gastropod shells washed up on sandy beaches may have lived out their lives in a range of habitats (grass beds, rocky shores, mangrove swamps, etc.). Where it is likely that these shells might be more easily found (alive or dead) on rock or mangrove, they will be covered in one of the next two chapters.

Fig 2.12 *These pieces are parts of a spiny lobster found on the strandline of a shore with coral nearby. The lobster most likely had a shelter on the reef.*

Fig 2.13 *The trumpet triton is a spectacular but not uncommon gastropod. This recently dead specimen was found in shallow water in Tobago.*

There are a number of fairly spectacular gastropods that turn up quite frequently. The **trumpet triton** is one such. In best condition much of the shell is covered with a wonderful pattern of gold and brown markings while the opening is marked on the outer side with lighter and darker patches and on the inner side with polished, sculpted ridges. Sadly the beauty of the shells is frequently marred by a covering of encrusting growths, often a thin layer of a seaweed (calcareous algae) that secretes a limy film on the surface. The opening is usually pristine due, of course, to the presence of the shell's owner. If the animal has been dead for some time and the shell has remained in the sea, even these areas will show signs of settlement by calcareous algae or small tubeworms. The similarly coloured but different shaped **tulip shell** lives in seagrass beds and appears on the strandline from time to time. Sadly it is rather fragile and beach washed specimens are often broken.

Conch shells of one sort or another are often encountered. Younger shells of the **queen conch** are quite tall with golden brown colouring on the outside and a rose coloured interior. The outer edge of the opening is thin and serrated. The magnificent shells of the adult are unlikely to be found on

Fig 2.14 *A collection of gastropods found on the strandline of sandy or coral rubble beaches in the British Virgin Island of Tortola. They are (clockwise from the top left) a very juvenile queen conch, West Indian fighting conch, tulip shell, five chestnut turban shells, a knobby triton, two netted olives and two cowrie helmet shells.*

Fig 2.15 *These mature queen conchs were first dumped on this Tobagan beach by fishermen after the meat (lambi) had been removed from the shells. Subsequent wear has resulted from the abrasive action of sand and mild wave action. Heaps of discarded conch shells are found wherever they are fished in any number.*

the beach unless they have been discarded by fishermen. The animal inside these shells (sometimes known as lambi) is used in a variety of conch stews and soups and shells are often sold by the roadside. The shells of those that have been caught and eaten can be distinguished by the cut through the upper part of the spire which releases the meat. The fully adult shell may be 30 cm (12 in) long and has a heavy flared lip. The inside of this lip and the opening are shiny and coloured with pinks and yellows. Three other smaller conchs that occur fairly commonly are the **West Indian fighting conch**, the **milk conch** and the **rooster tail conch**. The former has a yellow or orange outer colouring with an opening of orange sometimes overcast with a metallic grey. The lip does not extend upwards beyond the top of the opening. The milk conch has smaller spines than the fighting conch and, as its name suggests, the opening is a milky white but often stained with smoky grey. The rooster tail conch is easily distinguished by the pointed extension of the wing on the outer lip stretching well beyond the height of the shell's spire. In life the conchs move about with the opening (through which the foot protrudes) facing downwards. As they creep over the soft substrate upon which they live, the flared lip, characteristic of this group, gives some stability against being turned over by waves. Young queen conchs, which lack this lip, are not surprisingly known as 'rollers'.

Fig 2.16 *The rooster-tail conch is top left in this picture. Top right is the largest of the Caribbean cowries, the measled cowrie. As this animal grows its pale transverse bands get less obvious while the spots become more marked. Below this (bottom far right) are two Atlantic grey cowries and, to their left, two Atlantic yellow cowries. In the bottom left is a cowrie helmet shell.*

Three other fine shells to keep an eye open for are the **music volute**, the **reticulated cowrie helmet** and the **Atlantic partridge tun**. Music volutes gain their name from the markings on the shell, which suggest the lines and notes of sheet music. The reticulated cowrie helmet grows to a slightly larger size than the music volute (8 cm, 3 in) and has a large smooth area (the parietal shield) adjacent to the opening. Tun shells can reach up to 12 cm (5 in) and have fine chestnut and cream markings on their outer surface. The opening is large with spiral brown stripes.

Most of the gastropods you find will be smaller than those mentioned above but no less beautiful. Here are a few to look out for. The olives are long narrow shells usually highly polished and with fine reticulations on the outer surface. The opening is narrow and usually ridged on the body side. The **netted olive** is perhaps the most often encountered. Cowries are always much sought after. In these animals the shell develops so that the early whorls are hidden by the later ones so the usual spiral form, typical of many gastropods, is obscured. Thus the shell looks like a single chamber with a slit-like opening running the length of one side. Although large cowries occur in the Caribbean the beachcomber is much more likely to find the smaller forms especially the **coffee bean trivia** with its three pairs of dark brown spots and two cypraeas, the **Atlantic grey cowrie** and the **Atlantic yellow cowrie**. The first of these is more nearly brown despite its name and has paler transverse stripes while the latter has a whitish ground speckled with darker brown spots. All these cowries are about 1 to 3 cm ($\frac{1}{2}$ to $1\frac{1}{2}$ in).

Fig 2.17 *This picture is a fused image of the two faces of an Atlantic partridge tunshell, a not uncommon find on sandy beach tidelines.*

One occasionally finds the larger (to about 8 cm, 3 in) **measled cowrie**, which is so called because it usually bears white spots on a brown background (although some forms have pale transverse stripes rather than spots). One close relative of the cowrie is the **flamingo tongue**. In life this animal lives mainly on sea fans, browsing on the exposed tissue. The foot of this gastropod is cream coloured but it carries numerous black-bordered yellow spots. This foot covers most of the shell while the animal is feeding and, thus protected, its outer surface retains its very glossy appearance.

Superficially similar to cowries are the bubble shells. The resemblance is due to the fact that the final whorl of these shells also encloses the earlier ones. Closer examination shows that the opening is much larger than in cowries, especially at the lower end. The **striated bubble** is much the commonest species; fresh shells are light brown usually marked with darker mottlings. However this pigmentation is easily lost and older shells may be

Fig 2.18 *If you find a recently dead flamingo tongue shell it has a very shiny glaze due to the fact that in life it is mostly enveloped by the animal's foot. This relative of the cowries feeds on sea fans.*

Fig 2.19 *These gastropods were collected from sandy shores in Antigua. Clockwise from the top left they are: middlespined ceriths, brown moon shells (though in fact very white in these cases!), stocky ceriths, striated bubble shells and ivory ceriths.*

white, causing possible confusion with some other species which are white even in life. Another group of shells that loses its pigmentation quite quickly (and which also contains members that are white in life) is that containing the moon shells and naticas. These are true sand dwellers which spend their lives ploughing through the substrate in search of prey. The **naticas** are responsible for the small hole often seen in bivalve shells. The snail uses both chemical and mechanical means to drill this hole through which it inserts its proboscis in order to eat the mollusc flesh inside. Fresh natica shells are beautifully coloured in cream and honey browns but quickly lose their colour through abrasion by sand. The more solid **moon shells** are always white and are less fragile than naticas and consequently more common on beaches. Even more fragile are the beautifully coloured **violet sea snails**. Their shells have been reduced in thickness to enable them to float at the surface of the sea in a mass of bubbly mucus. These snails are predators of the Portuguese man-of-war, floating alongside it scraping away at the flesh with their rasping mouthparts. Because the shells are so thin they are mostly broken before arriving at the strandline; an intact specimen is a prize indeed. Like their prey, they are usually found on shores facing the prevailing wind.

Fig 2.20 *Shells collected from a sandy beach on the Atlantic (east) coast of Barbados. Clockwise from the left they are: Florida jewel boxes, mouse cones, Atlantic yellow cowries, common violet sea snails and coffee bean cowries.*

Fig 2.21 *In some places where there is virtually no wave action and the substrate is almost mud, algae will grow on the surface. These may be grazed by enormous densities of small gastropods. This example from Grenada shows ceriths (probably the awl miniature cerith) reaching populations in excess of 5000 per square metre.*

On very fine sands, which are almost muddy, the surface may be covered in small black spots, which, on closer examination, turn out to be snails. They feed either on strands of micro-algae or by scraping individual grains of silt for the algae and bacteria that live on their surfaces. Numbers may be astronomical; we estimated populations in excess of 5000 per square metre on one beach in Grenada. A variety of species may be involved but members of the sub-family Cerithiopsinae are most likely with the **awl miniature cerith** being one of the commonest.

The worm shells, a group of snails commonly found on the tideline, can at first be difficult to identify. They look more like a tangled mass of calcareous tubing reminiscent of those formed by some annelid worms. You may be lucky enough to find an intact shell of **Knorr's worm shell** that betrays it snail origins. In these specimens one can see that at first the animal possesses a small conically coiled shell similar to many snails. As it grows the coils of the shell separate from each other and lose their neat coiling, taking up a much more random growth pattern. In other species of worm shells the growth is even less ordered and the fragments found on the beach have a chaotic appearance.

Fig 2.22 *Worm shells are commonly washed up on sandy beaches. Despite their appearance they are in fact gastropods which, during growth, have abandoned the neat coiling of most of their relatives.*

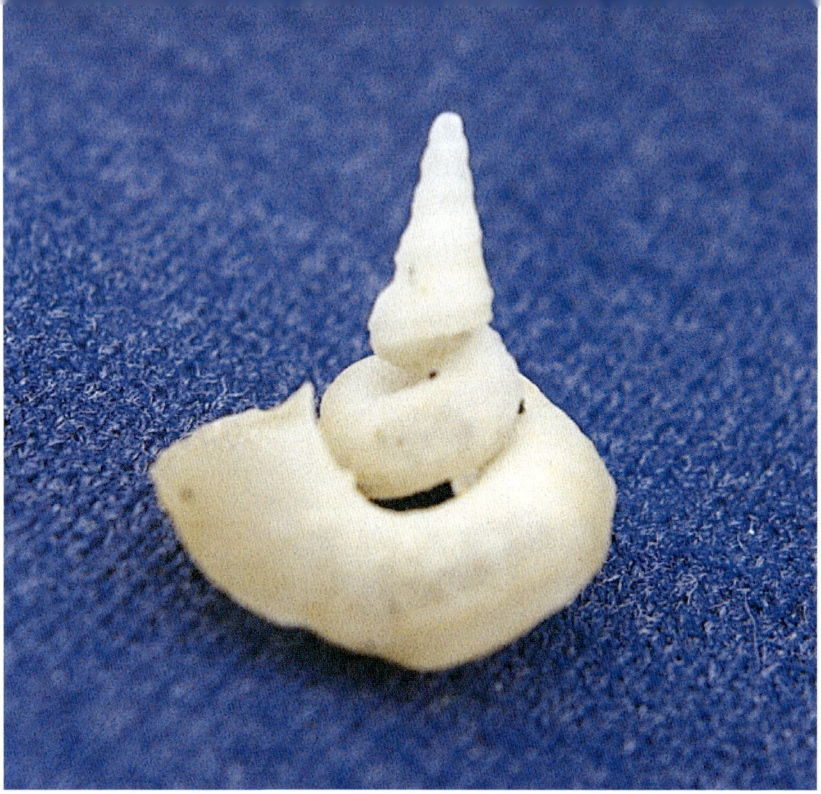

Fig 2.23 *You may be lucky enough to find an intact Knorr's worm shell that betrays the gastropod affinity of the worm shells. Notice how the shell starts out looking like a small snail of some sort. Only later in growth do the coils become detached from one another and adopt a more random pattern.*

Bivalve shells occur in huge variety on the strandlines of sandy beaches and afford the beachcomber endless fascination and satisfaction. As with gastropod shells, bivalve remains from a variety of habitats may turn up in the drift on a sandy beach. Those that are likely to be encountered alive on rocky shores or in mangrove swamps will be covered in Chapters 3 and 4 respectively.

A selection of the bivalves found on many beaches with moderate to high wave action is shown in Fig 2.24. These include the **Caribbean donax** known as chip-chip in many of the islands. This bivalve is sometimes extremely common, burrowing in the intertidal region of surf-pounded beaches. The larger tides of the southern part of the Caribbean region mean that enough of the beach is uncovered at low tide for this mollusc to be collected live and used in soups and other seafood dishes. Figure 2.24 also shows how variable bivalves can be in coloration and marking.

Figure 2.25 shows a collection from a somewhat more sheltered beach. Under these conditions lucines can be very abundant (in this case the **Pennsylvania lucine**). Their shells are thick and heavily built. In life this gives them stability against wave action and in death results in shells which are resistant to erosion by sand. These shells can survive being washed up and down beaches for much longer than the thinner and more fragile species.

This indicates that what we collect on the strandline has already been selected by nature with the more robust surviving and the more fragile being damaged or destroyed. What we find does not necessarily reflect very closely living inhabitants nearby. It is also worth mentioning here that erosion and fragmentation in shore-collected material can often lead to problems of identification. The action of sea and sand can remove key features and markings, sometimes making a safe identification impossible.

Fig 2.24 *These bivalves were collected at the beach of La Sagasse, Grenada. Down the left side are five gaudy aphis; down the centre are trigonal tivelas, including some intact pairs as in life; top right are six specimens, possibly tellins; middle right are five Caribbean donax or chip-chip with, bottom right, five pink microcockles.*

Similarly, to have only a part of the specimen may render naming impossible. This is clearly irritating in some cases but with experience the ability to put names to worn or broken bits has its own satisfaction. To those more concerned with aesthetics than taxonomy, fragments have their own charm, like the broken scallop shell in Fig 2.25.

Fig 2.25 *These were collected from Grand Anse, Grenada, a more sheltered beach than that of Fig 2.24. Many of the shells are heavily worn due to the abrasive action of sea and sand – often a problem with beach-collected material. Such wear sometimes makes definitive identification difficult or impossible. Shown here are a fragment of a six-hole urchin (top centre) with a coffee bean cowrie to its left and another cowrie (*Cypraea *sp.) to the right. Directly below the urchin is a beaded venus with a rigid venus to its left. Below the venuses are six heavily worn Pennsylvania lucines. Below the* Cypraea *are two small jewel boxes (*Chama *sp.), a fragment of scallop shell; below this are an eared ark (left) and a limpet (*Hemitoma *sp.) and below these five Atlantic strawberry cockles.*

Fig 2.26 *These three attractive species are found on quiet beaches often near mangrove swamps. Top, yellow cockle; lower left, cross barred venus; lower right, West Indian pointed venus.*

Scallops are bivalves that very clearly do not have two identical valves. The animal lies on the surface of the substrate, usually sand, with a flat valve uppermost and a much more convex valve beneath, lying partially buried. The animal feeds with the valves slightly open and the edge of the mantle slightly protruding along the frilly edge of which are a number of simple eyes. Should these detect a possible predator the valves will shut. For some scallops, more disturbance will lead to it swimming away by rapidly opening and shutting the valves. Water is thus alternately sucked into and blown out of the mantle cavity. The outward route is via spaces between the valves near the hinge and the animal progresses by a series of jerks with the hinge at the rear. This mode of swimming has been said to look like a 'demented castanet' and is provoked particularly by starfish, which are common predators of scallops. A very similar mechanism is employed by the **limas**, bivalves which also live unattached and on the surface of the seabed. They swim by a similar mechanism to the scallops but in the opposite direction so that the hinge is foremost. Like the scallops they also show a bright orange mantle when feeding.

Bivalves, which have limited mobility, often have adaptations to minimise being moved about by waves. One strategy is for the animal to attach itself to some solid object. They do this by secreting protein 'mooring ropes' called byssus threads, which are attached to the animal at one end and stuck very firmly to a rock or similar structure at the other end. Many do this and we will meet a number of them in the next two chapters. Some of the shells commonly found on shore strandlines have lived this way although the dead shells do not indicate it. The large group of ark shells and their relatives are good examples. The shells are commonly found and are often very distinctive. Best known, perhaps, is the **turkey wing** with its long, straight hinge line and rich brown and cream markings. Less striking but just as common in many places are the **white reticulated ark** and the **red-brown ark**. These shells can be good examples of pigment loss through wear, so when trying to identify them do not assume that a white shell was white in life.

Although some bivalves live free on the surface or attached, a great many spend their lives buried in sand or mud. Most of these communicate with the overlying sea water through a pair of tubes or siphons. Sea water is sucked in through one (inhalant) and pumped out through the other (exhalant). Inside the mantle cavity this sea water is passed through the large gills.

Fig 2.27 *A mixed bag from a beach in Tortola, BVI. Top left, both valves of an Atlantic wing oyster; top right, the foliate jewel box; lower right, a group of five turkey wings; lower centre, five worn valves of the Atlantic thorny oyster; lower left a 'coon oyster still attached to what is probably a branch of a sea plume together with a single valve of the same species.*

These organs act not only to take in oxygen but, much more importantly, also to sieve out organic particles (mainly microscopic plants, phytoplankton) that are the bivalves' food. In some bivalves the inhalant siphon is used like a vacuum cleaner to suck up detritus which may have settled on the surface of the sand or mud. Bivalve siphons poking up through sand offer a tasty snack to passing fish and to protect themselves the siphons often have a range of sense organs at their tips. If danger threatens the siphons are rapidly withdrawn.

Quieter waters where the sand is fine grained and perhaps there are seagrass beds offshore are a rich habitat for bivalves. One such inhabitant is the **amber pen shell**. This lives with most of its pointed end embedded in fine sand and the broad end protruding into the water. The shells are large but fragile and are only rarely washed up intact.

Cephalopoda is the name given to the group that contains octopuses and squids. These are molluscs but they mostly lack much (or everything) by way of a shell. **Squid** are mid-water creatures and will not be seen except perhaps from harbour walls and jetties. **Octopus** too sometimes turn up in shallow water on beaches but usually they are small, just a few centimetres across. However one representative of the group (the **common spirula**) does have a shell and it turns up on beaches regularly. Spirulas are squids which have a coiled internal shell divided into chambers by transverse partitions. In life most of the chambers are gas filled and the shell acts as a buoyancy device for this deep-sea animal. After death the shell is released and may well drift ashore.

Fig 2.28 *A full-grown amber pen shell. These large bivalves live with the pointed end of the shell embedded in the sand.*

Fig 2.29 *Sea urchin tests. Of course in life these urchins have spines covering the surface but they are quickly lost after death and the naked tests are often found washed up. Top centre, long-spined black urchin; top left and right, variable urchin; lower left and right, sea egg.*

Fig 2.30 *Sea egg shells discarded after having been opened by fishermen in order to remove the roes.*

Echinoderms are mainly represented on sandy shores by the shells (called 'tests') of sea urchins. Many urchins live on rocky shores but the **white sea egg** commonly lives on sand or seagrass beds. Occasionally the live animal is visible in shallow water at low tide. It is almost spherical with short white spines contrasting with the darker body. Like a number of other urchins, the sea egg deposits pieces of mollusc shell, seagrass or other debris over itself. The reason for this is unclear although camouflage may be the intention. The sea egg is fished commercially in some Caribbean islands, especially Barbados, as the reproductive organs are regarded as a delicacy. During the breeding season the testes and ovaries of the sea eggs are sloppy and soft but by late summer the release of eggs and sperm ceases and fat is stored in them. This results in their becoming much firmer and it is at this time that they can be scooped out of the animal and eaten, usually fried. They are delicious with a texture close to scrambled egg and a flavour all of their own.

A number of other urchins, the **sea potatoes** and **sand dollars**, live buried or partially buried in sand in shallow water and their tests will sometimes appear on beaches. Unfortunately they are rather fragile so intact specimens are unusual. In the typical urchin such as the sea egg the mouth is at the base of the animal close to the rock on which it grazes. The gut runs straight through and discharges via the anus at the top of the urchin. Because of their way of life the sea potatoes and sand dollars have tended to become more or less flattened and to develop a 'front' and a 'back' during their evolutionary history. The greater polarity of these animals is associated

Fig 2.31 *Two live six-hole urchins, close relatives of the sand dollars, in shallow water. The one on the left is just starting to bury itself in the substrate.*

with the fact that they plough through the sand always in one direction whereas the globular sea egg has no such preference. Another result of having a front is that the anus has migrated from the top (as it is in the sea egg) to the 'back' so that as the faeces are left behind they do not foul the animals' surface. The sea potatoes (including *Meoma* and *Echinoneus*) are moderately flattened, their height being about half their length while the sand dollar group, which includes the **common six-hole urchin**, are flatter, typically 8–10 cm (3–4 in) across but only about 1 cm (0.4 in) thick.

Turtles spend most of their lives in deep water but the females come ashore to lay their eggs. Sandy shores are the favoured sites for this activity. In recent years, thanks to increased conservation efforts and awareness, the opportunities to witness this event are much increased. A number of eco-tourism operations and hotels near turtle beaches now offer turtle watching to their customers.

Six species of turtle are known to breed in the Caribbean, namely **green, hawkshead**, **leatherback**, **loggerhead**, **olive ridley** and **Kemp's ridley**. Of these, the first three are more commonly encountered as breeding species. Their nesting seasons are roughly March to August with some species differences; in particular hawksbills may lay later into the year, perhaps even as late as December. The nesting behaviour follows a fairly similar sequence for them all. Females arrive at the chosen nesting beach and wait for darkness to fall. If they arrive before dusk you may well see them just offshore when their snouts break the water as they breath. Once it is fully dark turtles will emerge on to the beach, pushing their noses into the sand apparently testing it in some way. Assuming the female is satisfied, she climbs up the slope and on to dry sand. She may take some time to select a suitable site but eventually she will start to dig with her front flippers. Once she has a broad but fairly shallow pit she will switch to dig the deeper egg chamber with her hind flippers. This will be over 50 cm (19 in) deep and when it is completed she will proceed to lay her eggs, two or three at a time, for perhaps half an hour. Once laying is finished the hole is refilled with sand and the surface 'scuffed up' until the location of the pit is all but undetectable. Finally, the turtle moves back down the beach to the sea where she will feed and produce more eggs which will perhaps be laid a couple of weeks later. Leatherbacks are reported to lay about 80–90 eggs in each clutch with an average of 5–7 clutches at 9–10 day intervals. This amount of egg production is a considerable strain and it is generally thought that females lay only in alternate years or perhaps even less frequently.

The young turtles hatch and dig their way to the surface, usually at night. They orient themselves towards the sea on the basis that the sea's horizon is the lightest part of the sky and set off down the beach. At this stage they are very vulnerable to predation both on the beach and in the shallows and mortality is high. Another hazard is that any man-made light on the landward side of the beach (street lights, hotels, etc.) can produce disorientation and consequent failure to find the sea.

Fig 2.32 *These tracks were made by a female turtle as it crossed the beach before or after egg laying.*

Fig 2.33 *This photograph of a loggerhead turtle laying its eggs illustrates both the depth of the hole dug by the turtle and the large number of eggs laid during each visit to the beach.*

Box 2.1 Gastropods

These animals belong to one of the major subdivisions of the molluscs. The best known are the snails and limpets. Typically they have a single shell which in many cases shows spiral coiling. As the animal grows new shell is added to the coils in a clockwise direction when viewed from the top. Snail-like gastropods can retreat into this shell and in many cases have a 'door', the operculum, which closes across the opening to give extra protection. When the animal moves it protrudes the body out of the shell and glides over the surface by means of tiny muscular waves on the flat foot which is lubricated by the secretion of mucus. These muscular waves can be seen if the mollusc is persuaded to walk on a piece of clear glass so that the foot can be observed from below. As well as a large foot there is a clear head region that bears tentacles, which may have eyes at their tips. The mouth is usually invisible as it is on the lower surface close to the foot but again this can be seen if the animal is moving over glass. Inside the mouth many gastropods have a tongue-like structure covered in rows of sharp teeth. This is called the radula and is used to rasp and scrape food which may be anything from the microscopic algal film on rocks to live or dead animal tissue. In many of the predatory snails this radula is carried on the end of a long, extensible proboscis. The part of the animal's surface that produces the shell (and so is pressed against it) is called the mantle; over much of the animal there is a space between the mantle and the rest of its body which is called the mantle cavity. In this space are the gills of aquatic snails.

Some gastropods, especially the limpets, have an uncoiled shell which usually has a simple conical shape. When these animals move the soft parts remain covered by the shell so that the head and foot are not visible. Once again it is worth while to look at them walking on a piece of glass. In other respects they are much like the coiled shell snails.

Some groups of gastropods appear to be shell-less. This may be the case or it may be that the shell has become internalised, covered by overgrowing soft parts. Many of these animals (known by the general term of sea slugs) are brightly coloured although they are not often found by shore collectors.

Box 2.2 Bivalves

Another major group of molluscs is the bivalves. As their name implies, unlike the gastropods, they have two shells (often called valves) rather than one. In their simplest form the two valves are mirror images of each other, for example in donax. Often recently dead specimens will be washed up with the flesh missing (a snack for some hungry crab perhaps) but still joined by a structure called the ligament at the hinge region. As the shells grow material is added at the free edges away from the hinge; indeed this is clear in many shells which show concentric growth marks. Although some bivalves can move usually by 'clapping' the valves together, they are a largely sedentary group. Some bury themselves in sand or mud while others attach themselves to rocks or mangrove roots. A few have become borers and can dig into wood or even soft rocks. Inside the space between the valves is the animal itself.

The shell is secreted by a sheet of tissue, the mantle, which lines the valves. Part of the rest is a space, the mantle cavity, which is filled with sea water. This is typically drawn into the mantle cavity through a tube called the inhalant siphon and expelled through another, the exhalant siphon. Also in the mantle cavity are the animal's large gills which have a sieve-like structure and through which sea water passes en route from one siphon to the other. As the water moves through the gills, food particles are retained and caught in mucus. These are then passed to the mouth and eaten. Bivalves often have the ability to catch very small particles indeed, even as tiny as individual bacteria. The description above is a generalised one and the details may be different from species to species. In particular the exact arrangement of the mantle cavity and the currents through it vary a good deal. For those bivalves living deep in the sand the siphons have to be very long, and because of their bulk it may not be possible for them to be completely withdrawn into the shell. In these cases a pair of valves will not close completely and are known as gapers. In most species, however, complete closure is an important feature of their defence against predation. In order to hold the valves shut there are powerful muscles, usually two, attached at their ends to opposite valves. There are often marks on the valves showing where these muscles were attached.

Box 2.3 Echinoderms

Echinoderms are a common and important component of the marine fauna. Members of two sub-groups are especially easy to find on shores – sea urchins and brittle stars. Starfish and sea cucumbers are somewhat less common while the feather stars are deep-water forms not usually seen by beachcombers. The single most obvious characteristic of all five sub-groups is that they have a five-way symmetry. Thus starfish and brittle stars (usually) have five arms, urchins have five rays from top to bottom; even the sausage-shaped sea cucumbers often have five rows of suckered feet (called tube feet). In the simplest cases this symmetry is imposed evenly on a body form that has neither front nor back. In more complex examples some urchins and all sea cucumbers have developed a preference for one part to be anterior. In urchins this results from one of the five rays becoming dominant (as in sand dollars), but in sea cucumbers some of the rays form the underneath as if an urchin came to live on one of its sides.

The simplest form is to be seen in an urchin such as the purple rock borer. The animal has a mouth at the bottom close to the rock surface and the gut runs straight through to discharge via an anus at the top of the animal. On the external surface, running from mouth to anus, are five equally spaced rows of suckered feet that can hold the animal on to the rock but can also move in a coordinated way to take the urchin from place to place. The animal's skeleton is composed of the almost spherical shell (test) and numerous spines. Other suckered feet are arranged over the surface. Urchins that live in sand have become modified from this basic plan in the course of evolution. Thus the six-rayed urchin has become very flattened and the anus has migrated to the lower surface. This extra ray indicates the 'back' of the animal.

Brittle stars can be distinguished from starfish by having a discrete central disc and five spiny and relatively thin arms. They have tube feet but the animal moves mainly by vigorous movements of the arms and seems to be able to lead with any of the five. Starfish are relatively uncommon in Caribbean beach habitats but can be identified by the fact that there is no clear separation of the arms from the central disc. They have tube feet below and use them for walking.

3 Rocky Shores

Rocky shores offer considerable opportunity for seeing living animals and plants, not just washed up dead remains. As with sandy shores they will differ in exposure to wave action and in slope and geology. Additionally there are beaches composed of solid bedrock and those made up of boulders. Sand may also play its part either by its presence offshore or between the boulders, stones and rocky outcrops.

Zonation on rocky shores

There has been a huge amount of work worldwide investigating the ways in which animals and plants are distributed on rocky shores. In particular, much of this has been concerned with the sequence of organisms that can be observed as one moves down the shore from somewhat above the high tide mark to the low tide mark. At the various levels characteristic inhabitants can be observed enabling the shore to be divided into zones

Fig 3.1 *Castara Bay in Tobago. The tidal range here is about a metre at its greatest, large for the Caribbean. This photograph was taken at about low tide and the white zone (see text) marks the limit of high tide. The photograph also shows an example of a bedrock beach without undercutting.*

(often known by the names of their dominant plant or animal). Most of this research has been done in countries or regions where tidal ranges are larger than in the Caribbean but none the less the basic principles apply in our region despite its small tides. It is important to remember that this zonation results mainly from the amount of wetting that the various zones experience. Where wave action is a factor the splash and spray will produce a continuum from very wet to almost dry even in the absence of tides. Taking tides and waves together one can see that the zones will be most extensive when both tides and waves are large and most constricted when they are small. It is also obvious that slope will be important as the zones will each cover more area on a gently sloping shore than on, say, a vertical rock face.

The most widely accepted scheme applicable to rocky shores is Stephensons' three zone system (named after the husband and wife team, Alan and Anne Stephenson who gained unrivalled knowledge of zonation on shores around the world from the 1920s until the former's death in 1961). According to their research almost all rocky shores can be divided into a top zone (containing mainly lichens and small snails), a middle zone (dominated by barnacles and mussels) and a lower zone, which varies a good deal from place to place. This last is really an extension of the seabed from below the low tide mark and is only uncovered for short periods of time. The top zone can sometimes be divided into sub-zones on the basis of the colour of the rock; these sub-zones can be recognised in many places in the Caribbean. The highest is the white sub-zone where the rock is weathered and clean. This is a part of the shore where the influence of the sea goes furthest inland (apart from wind-borne spray). The animals that live here may be true land animals such as insects and spiders, or they may be marine creatures that have become more or less adapted to a terrestrial life, including crabs, snails and a woodlouse-like slater. These latter all have a dependence on the sea usually because they breed there and often have a swimming larval stage in their life cycles. Next down the shore comes a grey sub-zone with some seaweeds and a characteristic group of snails (in particular, many of the winkle species). More easily discerned is the black sub-zone which is usually covered at the highest tides. Its colour is probably due to a film of microscopic algae and it contains a number of seaweeds and is home to many nerite snails as well as the agile Sally Lightfoot crab.

The middle shore is also divided into an upper yellow and a lower pink sub-zone. In the former we find the highest (up the shore) populations of barnacles, mussels and limpets. The pink zone is so-called because of the coating of calcareous algae that covers the rock, and it is here that we encounter animals that can only survive for short periods out of sea water such as keyhole limpets, colonial anemones and some of the sea urchins. Below this we are into the lower zone in which we see animals and plants that are more reasonably regarded as truly marine but which can survive occasional exposure to air, including the zoanthids, the rock-boring urchin and the ark shells.

Fig 3.2 *This rock slab, also in Castara Bay, shows the sparse growth of seaweeds, especially if compared with similar sites in temperate zones. Wave action is mostly moderate at this site but larger waves wash over all of the weed on the slab even at low tide.*

Fig 3.3 *Three of the weeds that grew on the slab shown in Fig 3.2. Left,* Chaetomorpha *sp.; middle,* Dictyota *sp.; right,* Codium *sp. These weeds occupied zones on the slab with* Chaetomorpha *nearest the low tide mark,* Dictyota *in the middle and* Codium *highest of all. The dark spots on the* Chaetomorpha *are a minute, epiphytic red alga.*

Fig 3.4 *A boulder beach, also in Castara Bay. Note the pink zone of* Lithothamnium.

Fig 3.5 *There are a number of zoanthids that occupy the bottom of the intertidal zone, being uncovered only at the lowest point of the tide. These are related to sea anemones but are always colonial. This is the green zoanthid. Two others that are common are the mat zoanthid, which forms bluish-green colonies, and the yellowish brown knobby zoanthid.*

It is worth emphasising that the above description of zonation is a somewhat idealised one. In many instances it may be difficult or impossible to identify the sub-zones and on beaches with complicated topography the scheme may break down. Furthermore, on boulder beaches the complexity of the environment will confuse the simplistic concepts outlined above. In many parts of the Caribbean the very small tides might reduce the zones almost to nothing while the influence of wave action may frequently exceed that of tidal variation. It is worth noting that the Stephensons do not report from anywhere in the Caribbean, their closest examinations being in Bermuda and Florida where tides are generally larger than throughout the Caribbean. Much of the other research on zonation that has been applied to our region has had its origins in Florida or the Gulf of Mexico and so may not be strictly applicable. But to quote the Stephensons themselves, 'That zonations vary remarkably is an undoubted fact; they change... within a few yards on the same beach, clearly responding to local variations in the incidence of wave action and other controlling agencies. In spite of this ... however various the zonations may be, they are all variations on a fairly simple theme.'

Types of rocky shore and the importance of geology

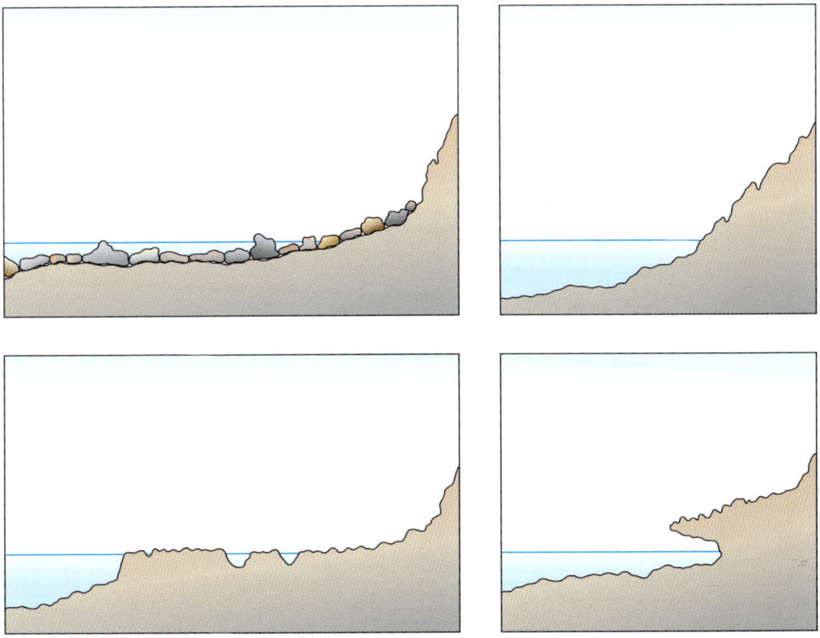

Fig 3.6 *Four examples of typical Caribbean rocky beach profiles. The upper left is a boulder beach (Fig 3.4), upper right is a hard bedrock beach showing little sign of erosion (Fig 3.1). Bottom left is a wave cut platform (Fig 3.7) and bottom right is an undercut rock face (Fig 8.1 on page 167). The bottom pair more often occur where the bedrock is soft (e.g. coral limestone).*

Bedrock shores vary considerably in their profiles. As has been mentioned in Chapter 1, the geology of the Caribbean islands is dominated either by relatively hard rocks of volcanic origin or by soft limestones (mainly fossil coral reefs). The former are fairly resistant to erosion by the sea and so shores composed of these rocks often depend on features of the local geology such as dip slopes and faulting. Where pieces are detached from the bedrock they can form boulder beaches with rocks that are stable and persistent. Bedrock beaches of coral limestone, in contrast, are quite rapidly eroded by wave action and, because of the small tides, this erosion is concentrated at one level. The result is typically one or more of two profiles: the rock is undercut or a small cliff is created in the sloping rock surface. Both of these may also have a flat, wave-cut platform on the seaward side at water level where the land has been removed by the sea over many years. The exposed surfaces of this type of rock become sculpted by the sea and various other agencies. The result is a micro-landscape of jagged, pitted and cleaved rock whose points and edges are fragile and razor sharp; not a place to investigate without adequate footwear nor one on which to be rolled over by a rogue wave. On the other hand it is a surface that offers many sheltering places for animal life, in particular snails, chitons and urchins.

Many rocky beaches are composed not of bedrock but of **boulders and smaller stones.** When pieces of coral limestone become detached from the bedrock they tend not to survive at the edge of the sea for very long and thus boulder beaches are not common where these soft rocks predominate. Exceptions to this occur in relatively quiet conditions where wave action is mild. Here coral rubble beaches develop with pieces of fossil coral mixed with recently dead coral from nearby reefs. In areas of harder rock, detached pieces

Fig 3.7 *A wave cut platform at Little Bay, east coast of Barbados.*

will collect on the shore, sometimes close to their place of origin but often having been moved considerable distances. Indeed many boulder beaches have rocks from a number of different geological sources. Weathering, sand and wave scouring will produce a range of surfaces from rough to polished, the former offering a greater variety of microhabitats. One of the most obvious features of boulder beach biology is that the inhabitants of the tops of the rocks are very different from those that live on the undersides. This is of course to be expected; those on the upper surfaces have to cope with wave action and the problems of the searing heat of the sun when exposed during daytime. In contrast those on the lower side are protected from both of these factors, remaining quiet, cool and damp. By turning the boulders one may find all sorts of interesting creatures. Some spend all their time under rocks while others simply shelter there, coming out to feed either after dark or at high tide. Although overturning rocks is a productive way of finding shore life it is vitally important to return the boulders to their original orientation. Failure to do this will result in the deaths of plants and animals on both sides as the delicate, damp-requiring inhabitants of the lower side will be exposed to the drying effects of sun and wind while those of the upper side become confined and compressed in darkness.

In the previous chapter it was noted that many sand dwellers spend their lives burrowing in the substrate. For those that live on rocky shores the need is to cling on for dear life for almost all such shores are washed by waves. To be detached and swept out to sea or crashed on to the rocks could be fatal. 'Clinging on' generally takes one of two forms. The attachment may be permanent with the animal or plant unable to move about on the substrate.

Fig 3.8 *Scorched mussels exposed to the full force of the sun during low tide.*

Alternatively, the organism may be able to hold on very tightly at some times while being capable of movement at other times. Animals such as barnacles and most seaweeds fall into the first category while limpets and chitons fall into the second. For many of the animals, the ability to hold their shell down tightly on to the rock surface is not only an adaptation to avoid being washed away but also to reduce desiccation to a minimum. When out of the water the drying effects of sun and wind can be extreme and, although many mobile animals will seek damp places to sit out the daytime hours, a tightly fitting shell will help to reduce water loss.

Fauna and flora

Sponges

The sponges most commonly found on the accessible parts of rocky shores are the encrusting forms that live on the undersurfaces of larger stones. These are usually only a few millimetres thick but often brightly coloured. Where space is available some may produce more upright forms. Identification of sponges is very difficult and usually requires a microscope to examine the minute spicules that make up the skeleton. As a number of them can sting when touched they are best left undisturbed. This is especially true of the **common red fire sponge,** which can cause painful burns, blisters and rashes.

Anthozoa (gorgonians, anemones and corals)

In still water (e.g. in marinas or harbours) hydroid colonies are relatively common on breakwaters and pilings. They have a feathery appearance and if examined closely it may be just possible to make out the tiny polyps which stand in lines on each of the branches. Like their other anthozoan relatives they possess stinging cells to help them to capture their plankton prey. In many species these are powerful enough to cause mild stings to unwary hands. Hydroids also abound attached to the leaves of sea grasses so try not to brush against them if you are swimming in the shallow waters of a seagrass bed. There are two coloured, encrusting zoanthids often uncovered at low tide. Superficially these look like corals (to which they are related) but are much softer to the touch. The form which is yellowish brown and has a cork-like feel is the **knobby zoanthid** while the bluey green, softer form composed of many anemone-like individuals is the **mat zoanthid**. Each of the individuals comprising these colonies is similar to a sea anemone but within the colony they are connected by basal tubes.

True sea anemones are less common than on temperate beaches although the **red warty sea anemone** is often found on rocks uncovered at low tide. This species has an orange or red column covered in vertical rows of paler warts. The oral disc with its white-blotched tentacles is frequently contracted during the day, opening only at night to reveal the characteristic red mouth.

Fig 3.9 *Hydroid colonies often establish on rocky shores but here they form part of the white encrustation on the leaves of seagrass. When these leaves are detached and washed up on the beach their various attached growths will probably still be visible. Notice also the three fanworms embedded in the sand. These filter feeding worms can often be seen when one is paddling in still, shallow water but will quickly retract their tentacles if disturbed.*

Another anemone, which is easy to identify, is the **pink-tipped anemone**. As its name implies the tentacles are tipped pink, purple or blue. These splendid creatures can attain diameters of over 30 cm (1 ft). The column varies in colour although pale blue and white are most usual. It mainly lives in deeper water but can often be seen attached to harbour walls and pilings.

Fig 3.10 *Pink-tipped anemone.*

Fig 3.11 *Some corals will grow in very shallow water, in particular the starlet coral,* Siderastrea radians.

Some corals are also found almost out of water on rocky shores. The commonest is one of the **starlet corals**, *Siderastrea radians*. This forms small, roughly circular colonies on rocks; they are characterised by their brownish colour and the many black dot- or slit-like openings where the polyps are situated. The **finger coral** is also to be found in shallow water and has upright colonies forming clumps of finger-shaped branches. The surface is closely covered with small, shallow depressions containing the polyps.

Annelid worms

If you are turning over stones on boulder beaches keep an eye open for the **green bristle worm**, sometimes called the fireworm. This is a flamboyant animal, mainly green but with red gills and white bristles on each segment. It can sometimes be seen on open rock surfaces in shallow water and would appear to be easy prey for passing fish. However, beware! The spines penetrate the skin of inquisitive fingers and can cause long-lasting irritation. It is this protection that gives the worm its confidence. There is a related **orange bristle worm** which is also a hazard to beachcombers.

Crustaceans

Crustaceans to be found alive on rocky shores include barnacles, crabs and their relatives. There is also one common relative of woodlice, the **beach slater**. These creatures live high up on beaches spending most of the day hidden beneath rocks, emerging at night to feed. If you turn over rocks during the day you may disturb them and catch a glimpse as they run swiftly to the nearest shelter. Usually about 25 mm (1 in) long they look rather like a small cockroach (indeed one of their common names is sea roach), but have many more legs (eight pairs) as well as two forked appendages at the rear.

Fig 3.12 *Goose barnacles attached to a piece of driftwood recently washed ashore.*

Fig 3.13 *Ribbed barnacles waiting for the tide to turn.*

Barnacles do not at first sight look like relatives of the scuttling, active crabs and other more typical crustaceans. The 'give away' is their larval stages which have all the hallmarks of true crustaceans. These larvae are planktonic but after some time living free in the sea they settle on to a hard substrate and take on their adult form. Barnacles fall into two major groups: the stalkless, hard-shelled barnacles so common on rocks and the stalked **goose barnacles** attached to floating objects such as the undersides of boats. The latter are most often found when they wash up on beaches attached to driftwood. Of the other group the easiest to identify is the **ribbed barnacle,** which is quite tall and conical, covered with fine ribs and grooves. Of the small stalkless species the **star barnacles** are probably the commonest forming crusts over intertidal rocks. These barnacles feed when the tide is up using their much modified legs to sweep plankton organisms and detritus out of the water. This feeding method can be easily observed by taking a small rock with barnacles on it and immersing it in sea water. After a few minutes the barnacles will usually open the plates and the legs will appear, waving in their characteristic way.

Of all the animals that typify the seashore the **crab** must be most people's choice. In the Caribbean the crab most often seen on rocky shores is the **Sally Lightfoot**. This crab earns its name by being nimble and fast moving. They frequent the water's edge sometimes submerged but not often dislodged by the waves. Their round bodies are as much as 8 cm (3 in) across with long legs usually stretched out on either side to grip the rock. The claws are relatively small and coloured red, contrasting with the body which appears

Fig 3.14 *A Sally Lightfoot crab caught unawares.*

Fig 3.15 *Two quite different crustaceans have the common name calico crab; this is one of them,* Eriphia gonagra, *which is frequent on rocky shores living in small holes and crevices.*

from a distance to be greenish grey. These claws have spoon-shaped tips and are used to graze on seaweeds. This handsome and common crab is difficult to get close to and even more difficult to catch as it is quite shy and watchful, darting behind rocks when approached. If surprised at close quarters it will leap abruptly into the sea where it appears to swim with ease.

Quite often one will come across the empty skin of Sally Lightfoot on the rocks. Sometimes these will be the result of predation (usually by birds) but more often these are shed skins. Crabs, like all other crustaceans, have hard outer skeletons and to grow they have to periodically shed this exoskeleton. The new one, which has been preformed underneath, is soft at first and allows the animal to expand for a short time until it hardens to form the new, larger covering. These moults permit close examination of the skeleton's intricate jointed structure and even the covering of the eyes will be visible. When crabs moult the skeleton splits around the edge of the body from the rear and the animal crawls out backwards. Thus if you find a crab skeleton where you can lift the back like a lid hinged at the front of the animal, you can be sure it is a moult. Often after death or moulting the skeleton of crustaceans will change colour to a much redder hue (as they also will when cooked).

Two other crabs found on rocky shores or under stones are the **spiny actaea** and the **calico crab**. The former has a broad body (about 25 mm, 1 in, across), short legs and rather stubby brown claws. The back is reddish and covered in spines and bristles. The calico crab is about the same size but has relatively larger claws which are bright yellow on the inner surface while the outer is covered with purple brown spots. It is an active little crab and can deliver a nasty nip if allowed.

Fig 3.16 *This dead (and somewhat incomplete) granulated spider crab has been washed up from deeper water.*

Fig 3.17 *This spotted sea hare is crawling almost out of the water. When fully immersed the flap-like parapodia down the back and the head tentacles expand and are much more obvious.*

Dead crabs are sometimes washed up from deeper water and quite often include **spider crabs**. These have bodies which are circular to triangular, often with two spines between the eyes. The claws have spoon-shaped tips and they and the legs are often covered with spines.

Molluscs

Rocky shores offer many opportunities to observe live molluscs rather than simply to collect dead shells. Indeed some of them lack shells anyway (or at least hide them away internally). Common among these shell-less forms is the **rough sea slug**, coloured in a range of hues from orange to brown. Its back is covered with many small, warty bumps in a contrasting, usually paler, colour. **Sea hares** are also not uncommon in rock pools and shallow water. Most species in this group have a fragile internal shell covered by two long flaps of tissue which forms a groove down the back. The head bears four flap-like tentacles, two of which are often large and because they look like ears give these animals their name. **The spotted sea hare** emits clouds of purple ink if disturbed, presumably as a defence mechanism.

Limpets abound on most of the rocky shores in the region. They have simple conical shells and fall into two basic groups: those with a slit at the apex of the shell (keyhole limpets) and those without. Under the shell is an animal much like other gastropods, its anatomy dominated by the muscular foot.

Fig 3.18 *Limpets are common alive on rocky shores and their shells frequently occur on beaches. All of these were found in a few minutes at Little Bay on the east coast of Barbados. The small white shell in the middle is Goe's false limpet; the others are, clockwise from the left, the dwarf suck-on limpet, the green keyhole limpet, the Barbados keyhole limpet, the eight-ribbed limpet and the knobby keyhole limpet.*

Fig 3.19 *The West Indian top shell is common on rocky shores. Large specimens may be as much as 10 cm (4 in) across.*

When out of the water the foot clamps the limpet to the rock surface making it almost impossible to remove without damage. As the animal has its own personal home site the shell will have grown to fit even the subtle indentations in the rock so predators find it all but impossible to remove them from the substrate. Under water or in damp night conditions the limpets will crawl about much like a snail. Once on the move and away from their home site they are much easier to remove and so more susceptible to predation. Their usual means of feeding is by scraping the microscopic algae from the rock surface using their file-like mouthparts (radula). The slit in keyhole limpets is the exit pore for water currents that the animal creates. Water enters around the periphery of the shell, passes over the gills and past the anus and thence out of the slit carrying away solid waste and carbon dioxide. Both groups are common dead and alive and the shells of a number of species are illustrated in Fig 3.18.

When searching among loose stones, rock pools and bedrock beaches you will come across many **snails** having the familiar coiled shell with its opening (aperture) often sealed up with a 'door' (operculum). This classic body form is perhaps typified by one of the commonest shore snails, namely the **West Indian top shell**. This animal can grow to be as much as 10 cm (4 in) across but those found near the water's edge are usually smaller than this. The shell is heavy and marked black and white on the outside. The inside of the aperture has a wonderful opalescent sheen as do worn parts of older or sand-scoured shells. This snail is still widely eaten in the Caribbean, usually on the beach, so it is not uncommon to come across small piles of freshly broken shells (usually accompanied by beer bottles or cans); a sure sign of an impromptu barbecue. Much smaller but no less beautiful are the tegulas of

Fig 3.20 *Three very common gastropods of rocky shores. From the left, the wide-mouthed purpura, the tessellated nerite and the green-base tegula.*

Fig 3.21 *Star shells at sunset. The oblique lighting and shadows indicate the relative heights of these three shells which are (from the left) the carved star shell, the green star shell and the long-spined star shell.*

which the **green-base tegula** is a commonly found example often clustering by the hundred in pools or damp depressions in the rocks. These snails, which are about 12 mm (0.5 in) across, have the aperture placed in a very flat base to the shell in the middle of which is a small hole or depression called the umbilicus. The area around the umbilicus is coloured a pearly green while the rest of the shell is brown with darker mottling. Relatives of the tegulas include two other common groups of snails – the turbans and the star shells. The **chestnut turban** is usually a light reddish brown in colour with white spots and a crisp sculpturing of dots and low ridges. The star shells form a nice series from the tall relatively smooth **imbricated star shell** through the squatter **green** and **carved star shells** to the almost flat and dramatically shaped **long-spined star shell**.

Fig 3.22 *Older books would identify most of these small shells as the zebra winkle. However, that species has been extensively revised and subdivided into a number of new species (see text). The three larger, black shells (two upper left, one lower right) are the black Atlantic planaxis.*

Fig 3.23 *The beaded periwinkle is not only found on upper shore rocky environments but will also settle on twigs and branches above the high tide mark.*

High up on Caribbean rocky shores and continuing down to the low tide mark there are many species of winkles. These beautiful little snails (mostly less than 25 mm, 1 in) are often difficult to identify with certainty. In particular, the species called the **zebra periwinkle** is now known to be in reality at least four closely related species. To make things more difficult, they are somewhat variable in form. Do not be daunted for with a bit of careful observation it is possible to put a name to most of them. Like many shore molluscs they are zoned (see page **53** above). At the very top of the beach, as much as 10 m (30 ft) above sea level, is the **beaded periwinkle**. Its shell is conical, whitish grey and covered in regular rows of rather similar sized beads. It is often relatively large, up to 25 mm (1 in). The base of the shell is fairly flat and also beaded. High above sea level, this species is often found attached to twigs of trees and the like. Slightly lower down the beach (but still well above the high tide mark) are two other greyish beaded species, the **common prickly-winkle** and the **false prickly-winkle**. In both these species the sculpted beads are of rather variable size, with a double row of large ones at the widest part of the shell. Of these two, the former species looks taller while the latter has a more squat shape. The former also has a 'shelf' interrupting the entry of the opening, which in the latter is perfectly smooth. The false prickly-winkle seems to be very dependent on crevices and pits in the rock surface for shelter and is often absent from smooth rock beaches. Also at this level is one of the species previously lumped together as zebra periwinkles, namely *Nodilittorina angustior*. This is an elegant smooth winkle with bold black and white stripes running fairly straight and uninterrupted down the shell. Lower still is another of the zebra periwinkles (*N. ziczac*) (although it tends to overlap with the lower end of the distribution of *N. angustior*). *N. ziczac* can be quite large (up to 25 mm, 1 in) and is smooth but pale; when stripes are present they are faint compared with those on *N. angustior* and follow a zigzag course down the shell. Lower still down the beach is another of the zebra group, *N. interrupta*, which is often to be found on shores where mud is mixed with stones and rocks. The reason for the name is that the black and white lines running down the shell are interrupted by wide black bands spiralling round each whorl of the shell; sometimes these bands take over and the shell is almost totally black except for a few white spots on the base.

Much easier to identify are tiny winkles that occur almost at the low tide mark, usually on quiet, sheltered beaches. These **spotted periwinkles** have beautiful shells of black covered with tiny white spots. There is also another, the **dwarf periwinkle**, where the marking is reversed with black spots on a white background. This species also occurs in an unspotted yellow-brown form. Neither of these species exceeds 7 mm ($\frac{1}{3}$ in).

As always there have to be a few misleading specimens. The one you are most likely to come across is the **black planaxis**, a winkle-sized snail with an all-black shell. Careful examination shows that, unlike the winkles, it has grooves in the shell on the lower outside of the opening. The opening also has a groove at its junction with the columella rather like a siphonal canal. There is a similar **striped planaxis** but in this case, as the name implies, the shell is striped brown and white.

Another very obvious group of snails that live on rocky shores at the water's edge are the nerites. These are mostly rather larger than the winkles and all of them are characterised by a flat area on the inner wall of the opening (the parietal area). This is often stained or has teeth which help to identify the individual species which all live, often together, on rocks between the tidelines. The three commonest species are shown in Fig 3.26 and are fairly easily distinguished. Easiest of all is the **bloody-toothed nerite**, so-called because it has three white teeth surrounded by a blood-red staining. The rest of the shell is highly variable with a range of stripes and blotches of reds, browns and black. The **four-toothed nerite** looks very similar on the outer surface of the shell as you see it sitting on the rocks but

Fig 3.24 *Tessellated nerites clustered into shallow depressions on a rocky shore to exploit any dampness available.*

Fig 3.25 *A group of bloody-toothed and four-toothed nerites (with one tessellated, left). These two species are highly variable and occur together on the shore. They cannot be reliably identified without turning them over to examine the parietal area (see Fig 3.26). Note the various winkles sheltering in the depressions.*

turn it over and immediately one sees the totally white parietal area with four teeth. The third species, the **tessellated nerite**, has only two rather feeble teeth on its parietal area and is usually identifiable by its checked black and white shell (although sometimes black tends to dominate the pattern).

Another common shore snail which might be found either alive clinging to low shore rocks or as a dead shell in drift is the **wide-mouthed purpura**. In life the shells are well camouflaged, blending with their background. If removed from the rock the animal will exude a purple fluid which will stain the skin; presumably this is an anti-predator response. The inside of the shell is a rich, warm, chestnut brown.

Many snails have a long siphon that can be extended from the shell when they are moving. The siphon, which communicates with the mantle cavity, is largely sensory testing the water ahead and 'sniffing' the substrate. To permit the siphon to extend out of the shell these snails have a tubular fold at the base of the opening of the shell called the siphonal canal. In some cases the canal will close over and become a tube rather than a groove.

Fig 3.26 *The three common nerite species can be easily identified by the appearance of the parietal area (see text for explanation). Upper, tessellated; lower left, four-toothed; lower right, bloody-toothed.*

Fig 3.27 *Some shells from Little Bay, Barbados. Clockwise from the left, Lister's tree oyster, gold-mouthed triton, wide-mouthed purpura, smooth dove shell, fragments of various chitons and West Indian top shell.*

About half the species of snail found in the Caribbean have such a canal and its presence and form are important features in identification. One common group of rocky shore snails with a siphonal canal is the ceriths and their relatives. Mostly they are relatively tall and pointed, about 20–25 mm ($\frac{3}{4}$–1 in) long. Not infrequently the dead shells are taken up by small hermit crabs so if they run away when you try to pick them up do not be surprised. Judging by the fact that many have broken openings we suspect they are commonly preyed upon by larger crabs. Another group of snails with siphons are the **tritons** and **frog-shells**. These have heavy shells, often with thickening around the opening and longitudinal ribs running down the spire of the shell.

You may well come across cone shells although more usually they will just be dead beach-worn specimens. This group is characterised by shells with a very shallow, almost flat, spire but with a large last whorl which has a markedly conical shape (with the point at the base of the shell). The opening is long and narrow. These shells may be brightly coloured and individual species are often variable in pattern and hue. The **mouse cone** is common all around the Caribbean. It has a medium sized shell, about 25 to 35 mm (1 to 1$\frac{1}{2}$ in) in length and usually grey with brownish mottling. On the shoulder of the shell there are a number of white knobs. Less common but more spectacular are the **West Indian alphabet cone** and the **glory of the Atlantic cone**. The former is larger than the mouse cone (up to 6 cm, 2$\frac{1}{2}$ in), white in colour but with spiral rows of reddish brown spots and blotches. The latter is slightly smaller and varies in colour from pinkish white to red with brown blotches distributed mainly in the middle of the whorl.

Fig 3.28 *Dove shells and cantharus are often extremely common and frequently used in locally produced craft items. Top right in this picture is the common dove shell with a group of common cantharus below; lower centre is a single smooth dove shell. Also shown is a group of hoof shells (lower left). The shells in the upper left are land snails (*Pleurodonte isabella*) that live in the gullies near the beach. During heavy rain they are washed out to sea and then eventually reappear on the beach.*

The cones are carnivorous snails catching even fast moving prey such as fish. Most gastropods have a belt-like structure (the radula) in their mouths covered with rows of teeth. The radula is usually used to rasp plant or non-mobile animal food but in cones the individual radula teeth have become harpoons loaded with venom produced by the digestive system. These teeth can be shot into fish or other prey which are paralysed. The prey is then ingested whole. These radula teeth can also be used in self-defence so live cones should be handled with care. Caribbean species probably do not pose a threat but human fatalities have occurred from Pacific and Indian Ocean species.

Chitons are very common members of the rocky shore fauna usually living on rocks at the low tide mark or in rock pools. These molluscs have a flat foot much like that of the limpets but one can immediately see that it is not a snail as the shell is composed of a set of eight saddle-shaped plates arranged down the length of the animal. These primitive molluscs feed by scraping algae and detritus from the rock surface using a radula rather similar to that of snails. The live animal is easily observed and identified but after

Fig 3.29 *Two spectacular cone shells are shown here, the alphabet cone (bottom left) and the glory of the Atlantic cone (bottom right). The other shells are two chestnut latirus either side of a damaged triton (top row) and a green star shell (lower centre). The coin, for scale, was also found on the beach, polished by sea and sand to a featureless disc.*

death the individual shell plates become separated and are commonly found on beaches. The front and back plates are roughly semicircular while the six plates between are narrow V-shaped strips of shell; simple when you know but often enigmatic on first viewing.

Rocky shore **bivalves**, unlike their sandy shore relatives, have to hang on to the substrate rather than dig into it. As in temperate regions the commonest such bivalves are mussels. In the Caribbean there are two species which are common, the **yellow mussel** and the **scorched mussel**. They are both relatively small at about 25 mm (1 in) and 18 mm ($\frac{3}{4}$ in) respectively. The yellow mussel, as its name implies, has a yellow shell while the scorched mussel is yellowish brown to dark brown, at least in life. The pigmentation is in a protein layer (called the periostracum) that covers the shell. After death, and even to some extent during life in older shells, this can wear away, sometimes breaking off like ageing nail varnish. Thus beach worn shells without the periostracum are more difficult to identify. In these cases one can usually rely on the scorched mussel being smaller, broader and darker than the yellow mussel and with some metallic purple on the inside of the shell.

Fig 3.30 *This common West Indian chiton shows the typical structure of six articulating valves and a further semicircular valve at each end. This movable shell protects the soft parts of the animal and has a striped girdle around the edge.*

Fig 3.31 *Some chitons, such as this fuzzy chiton, are well camouflaged. The name comes from the characteristic fuzzy, black and white girdle. Note the zoanthid polyps (top right) and the barnacles (left).*

Also commonly found attached to rocks is **Lister's tree oyster** (not such an inappropriate name as it is also found on mangrove roots). This small (about 25 mm, 1 in) oyster is often found closely packed so that the flat shells protrude from the surface like edge to edge coins. The shell is variable in colour from dark red to black with chalky mottling. The inside of the shell has a pearly opalescence and is immediately identified by the presence of four to eight square-shaped grooves at the hinge, where the two valves join (Fig 4.22). The **Atlantic pearl oyster** is also common on rocky shores; in this case the name is inappropriate as it very seldom harbours pearls! It is easily identified by the long straight hinge line. While on the subject of oysters, keep a look out for the interesting **'coon oyster**. The two valves of this mollusc close along a very pronounced zig-zag line so that each valve has a number of sharp points along its margin. Your best chance of finding this bivalve is by examining cast up sea whips and sea fans to which they are usually attached.

Fig 3.32 *All of these bivalves turn up in beach collections but only one, the yellow mussel, lives on rocky shores. These are, clockwise from the large shell in the top centre, the thick lucine, yellow mussels, the princess venus (very worn), the pink thin tellin and the king venus.*

Many other bivalves live attached to rocks but most of them occur below the tidelines and are not easy to find from the shore. However, many of them occur as beach-worn specimens and have been covered in the previous chapter.

Echinoderms

This group is well represented on rocky beaches mainly by sea urchins and brittle stars.

Two species of **sea urchin** commonly found in depressions in the rock are the **green rock borer** and the more common **purple rock borer**. The former has spines which are green tipped with purple while the latter has dark spines varying from dark red through purple to almost black. Both occur in holes and clefts in rocks at about the low tide level often in large numbers. Their spines are relatively short and blunt and they can be handled safely if a little care is taken. Like most rocky shore urchins they feed by rasping the surface of the substrate using the hard plates of their complex mouthparts to graze algae. If you find a recently dead specimen washed up the jaws may still be in place but can easily be removed and examined. The structure, known as Aristotle's lantern, like the urchin, has a fivefold symmetry and is worked by muscles attached to various parts of the lantern and to the inside of the shell. On soft rocks the constant action of the jaws can erode the surface giving these urchins their name.

Fig 3.33 *The purple rock borer urchin is common on the intertidal and shallow water sections of rocky shores.*

Fig 3.34 *This is the test (shell) of a dead purple rock borer urchin, the spines having fallen away. The mouth would have been on the underside. The mouthparts (Aristotle's lantern) have been removed and can be seen below the test; the pointed end contains the five teeth that scrape algae off the rocks.*

The best known (and much feared) urchin of rocks is the **long-spined black urchin**. This lives much more out in the open than the borers and has a complete covering of purple or black needle-sharp spines. Beachcombers will not usually see it as its normal habitat is below the low tide mark. However, in quiet water conditions and at low tide they can sometimes be observed in the shallows and swimmers may encounter them. The spines are able to penetrate a person's skin even if lightly touched and the broken tips remain as small black dots. The spines, like those of all urchins, are covered with live tissue, which in this case contains a toxin that causes considerable irritation. Remedies abound from lime juice (to dissolve the spine) to meat tenderisers (to break down the toxin). Our own view is that rum taken internally is as good as anything! Altogether safer is the edible **white sea egg** which usually lives in deeper waters but edges up towards the beach on some occasions. The **pencil urchin** (Fig 3.35) is unmistakable due to its long but very blunt spines that are light brown in colour but often encrusted with algae. It is fairly common under stones at or below the low tide mark.

Brittle stars are often found under rocks at or near the tideline. For people who know these animals from temperate regions, the speed at which they move in the tropics will come as a surprise. No sooner is the stone overturned than they are away, five lanky arms thrashing as they head for the nearest cover. This group of echinoderms can be distinguished from their relatives, the starfish, by the fact that the central body is small and flattened while the very mobile arms are long, slender and often bear spines and visible plates. There are many species but **ophiocomas** are common under stones. These large brittle stars (15 cm, 6 in, across the arms) have stout spines and are black or shades of dark red. Brittle stars feed in various ways but most either filter plankton and detritus out of the water using their arms or gather similar small particles from sand and rocks.

Fig 3.35 *The pencil urchin with its thick, stubby spines is easy to identify. Often found under rocks this one has been placed in the open to be photographed.*

Sea cucumbers are sometimes to be found in rock pools or under stones. These animals seem unlikely members of the echinoderm group, most of which clearly show their fivefold symmetry. This is much less obvious in the external appearance of these rather sausage-like animals. However, in one case (**Agassiz's sea cucumber**) the five calcareous plates around the anal opening do show this typical echinoderm feature and also identify this particular species as no other species in the Caribbean possesses them.

Seaweeds are not such a feature of Caribbean beaches as they are for those of temperate regions. None the less they do occur attached to solid substrates and washed up on sandy and rocky shores. Below the low tide mark they are important members of the community and, because of the strong light and relatively clear water, occur to considerable depths.

Those found on shores or in shallow water belong to a range of genera but a few are particularly common. Of the green algae, the flat, soft blades of the **sea lettuce** are often found where there is fresh water influence especially if this is combined with nutrient enrichment. *Enteromorpha* is a simple tubular alga that sometimes grows on the surface of sandy mud; it

Fig 3.36 *The spiny ophiocoma is one of a number of brittle stars to be found under rocks in the intertidal zone or in shallow water.*

Fig 3.37 *Sea cucumbers are occasionally found on rocky shores. This is Agassiz's sea cucumber; it is easily identified by the presence of five plates around the anal opening (not visible in this photograph).*

may be the weed which is visible in Fig 2.21 on page 38. A larger and very common green alga is *Halimeda*. When alive it has the form of chains of bright green beads or discs but after death the living tissue rapidly disappears to leave the bleached white calcareous skeleton. There are a number of closely related species. Two other examples of green algae are shown in Fig 3.3 on page 55.

Fig 3.38 *A view of a small rock pool housing a number of seaweeds and two urchins. Linked locules of* Halimeda *are visible draped over the upper urchin and in the lower left. On the right, near the upper urchin, are two banded weeds: the smaller semicircular one is* Padina *while the longer somewhat split one is* Stypopodium. *The black filaments left of centre are probably the red alga,* Gelidium. *At least one unidentified green alga is visible as a fuzzy growth in a number of places.*

Perhaps the commonest of the brown algae is *Padina* which, like *Halimeda*, has a range of species all with a calcareous skeleton. This weed has a characteristic fan shape, often twisted into a cup. The blade is clearly marked with concentric lines and is tan coloured while alive but bleaches white when detached. A very similar weed is *Stypopodium*. This also shows the concentric markings but has longer blades which tend to split at the upper margin. It can also be distiguished from *Padina* in that it is not calcified and lacks the in-rolled margin characteristic of the latter. The other extremely common brown alga is *Sargassum* (Figs 1.11 and 3.40 on pages 13 and 85, respectively). Two species spend their entire lives floating in the open sea while another three or four are found attached to rocks, often in dense stands. All occur as part of the tideline debris. Another brown alga is shown in Fig 3.3 (page 55).

The red algae that most often come to the notice of the beachcomber are, once more, calcareous species. On many rocky shores the bedrock and stones may be coloured pink by a thin film of the encrusting alga *Lithothamnium* while the tangled limy skeletons of other reds, such as *Amphroa*, are frequently washed up.

Fig 3.39 *A clump of* Padina *washed up on the beach still attached to a piece of dead coral.*

Fig 3.40 *A tapestry of seaweeds and purple rock borer urchins in shallow water. The weeds are* Sargassum *(the browner form) and* Padina *(the paler fan-shaped fronds).*

Fig 3.41 *The calcareous red alga,* Lithothamnium, *coats not only this rock but also partially covers the ribbed barnacles that are attached to it colouring both pink.*

Box 3.1 The Seaweeds

Seaweeds belong to a group of primitive plants called Algae. They can be divided into three groups by the pigments that they contain. The groups are green, brown and red algae. They come in an enormous range of physical shapes and sizes from single cells to very large elaborate plants with leaf- and stem-like structures. However, they do not have roots. Those that are sedentary, either attached to rocks or in the sand, or epiphytic (attached to other plants) have a structure called a holdfast. Some algae, especially in the green group but also a few red species, have an internal or external jointed crystalline skeleton made of calcium carbonate or silicate. Once dead, these make an important contribution to sand. Finally, there are a group of red algae, the coralline algae, that do not look like plants at all but like dabs or sheets of pink or red or purple paint attached to rocks or other hard surfaces below the water.

The distribution of different species is controlled by the type of substrate as well as the ability to survive periods of exposure to the air, the influx of fresh water and the depth of the sea water.

Box 3.2 Crustacea

Crustacea belong to the larger group Arthropoda. All of these animals have a hard external covering. As well as protection this acts as a skeleton, supporting the body and having muscles attached to it for movement. Of course movement requires that the external skeleton has joints; these can be easily seen, for example, in the leg of a crab. One problem for arthropods is that growth is limited by the rigid skeleton. Thus these animals increase in size by shedding their skeleton, emerging in a softened and 'stretchy' skin. They rapidly increase in size for a short time before this new skin hardens to form the new external skeleton. During this short period of moult the animals are vulnerable as they are not only poorly protected but also unable to move effectively. Despite these limitations the phylum Arthropoda is extremely successful and contains more species than any other comparable group. The most widespread and diverse arthropods are the insects although other sub-groups include spiders and the crustacea.

Crustaceans are mainly aquatic although the terrestrial woodlice can live in damp environments. In marine (seawater) habitats the best known crustaceans are crabs. These all have four pairs of legs and a pair of pincer-like claws. The hind part of the body (abdomen) is curled underneath the section with the legs (thorax) so that crabs tend to be short and wide. In their close relatives, the shrimps, prawns and lobsters, the abdomen is extended giving a body form that is much more elongated. Many of these animals have much less obvious claws than crabs. Hermit crabs have taken to protecting their abdomens inside discarded snail shells. As a result their structure has become considerably distorted to fit the shell but their crab-like affinity can easily be seen in the typical claws. Two other groups of crustaceans not mentioned in any detail in this book include the woodlice relatives (slaters) and the sand hoppers. Mostly these animals are small and easily overlooked but they are in reality both common and important in shore and marine habitats. Barnacles are also crustaceans as can be suspected by the fact that their legs (which sometimes can be seen protruding from their shells) are jointed just like other crustaceans. However, the most convincing evidence comes from their reproductive cycle. Obviously the adults are attached to rocks and so are unable to move but the young stages (larvae) live in the open sea for some time before settling. In this free-living stage they have many of the characteristics of typical crustaceans. Their metamorphosis into adult barnacles is almost as startling as the change from caterpillar to butterfly.

4 Mangrove Swamps

Of the three major Caribbean shore environments, mangrove swamps are the least well known by the non-specialist. This is due in part to their lack of glamour compared with sand and rocky beaches and in part to difficulties of access. However, the ecological importance of these swamps is becoming more widely understood as their particular splendour is experienced by more and more people. Throughout the region the major swamps are being opened up to visitors and even remnants are being conserved. Increasingly, the research that has revealed the value of these habitats is being heeded. None the less destruction of mangrove swamps continues in the name of progress.

Mangrove swamps are defined by the presence of certain trees (not surprisingly called mangroves!). In the Caribbean there are three or four species of such trees that might be considered as mangroves but at least one of these can also grow in a range of non-swampy conditions.

Fig 4.1 *Mangrove swamps tend to be regarded as unattractive places that are not worth visiting. These are largely false impressions as the best are beautiful and rewarding places and even the smallest offer examples of fascinating flora and fauna. This lagoon is in the swamps near Port Royal in Jamaica's Kingston Harbour.*

The typical mangrove swamp is on gently shelving ground at the edge of the sea or on the banks of tidal estuaries. Wave action is not usually vigorous and mud may be being deposited. The water is salty, often undiluted sea water, although it may be mixed with river water or runoff from the land. The swamps will develop with their characteristic trees zoned so that the most water tolerant species will be on the seaward side, perhaps with their roots in standing water, and those less able to cope with inundation growing on higher ground further back. In less favourable conditions perhaps a few individual trees of a single species will be growing on more rocky or exposed beaches. In some cases these few will be the first colonisers heralding the beginnings of a larger stand; in other situations they may be the last pathetic survivors of previously larger groves.

Trees

There are four species that are common in West Indian mangrove swamps; you may not find them all in any given swamp although there are plenty of places where you will.

Fig 4.2 *Flowers and leaves of red mangrove.*

Fig 4.3 *Mature fruits of red mangrove. Note the already developed seedling root.*

Red mangrove

This is the commonest mangrove and the easiest to identify. It is the most water tolerant of the trees and usually grows with its roots in water. Well established, older trees may grow to about 9 m (30 ft) but they are often only half that height or less. One of the most obvious features of red mangroves is their prop roots. These arch out from the trunk well above water level and are clearly an adaptation to growing in a wet and fairly unstable environment that might be sometimes subjected to waves; these trees need a broad and stable base. Higher up in large red mangroves other roots grow out from branches and hang down in an elaborate tracery. The elliptical leaves are a shiny dark green with a thick leathery texture. The flowers are yellowish cream with four petals and are borne in small groups.

The fruits are extraordinary in that the seed inside starts to grow while still attached to the parent plant and by the time it is shed the main root of this new plant (called a propagule) is some 15 cm (6 in) long and as thick as a pencil. When the fruit becomes detached it will usually fall into water where it floats, often vertically. Eventually it may be washed ashore where the root will start to penetrate the soil and a new tree is established. If the propagule falls directly on to mud or drier soil it may penetrate like a falling arrow and start its independent life that way.

In a mature mangrove swamp, the red mangrove zone becomes an almost impenetrable tangle of stems, trunks and prop roots. This mass of vegetation is a very effective trap for falling leaves and water-borne debris that over time builds up. The consequences of this are many and of considerable environmental importance. Firstly, the accumulation will eventually become so great that the swamp will begin to emerge from the water and new land will be created. Secondly, the detritus soup between the prop roots is rich in nutrients and supports complex and productive food webs. Because of this (and also because the physical complexity of the mangrove roots acts to deter large predators) swamps are nurseries for many animals that live as

Fig 4.4 *Once in a suitable site the red mangrove propagules rapidly grow into small trees.*

adults in deeper waters or on reefs. Thirdly, the mud and detritus have the ability to capture and bind a range of microorganisms and potentially toxic chemicals that may otherwise enter the sea from the land or adjacent rivers. Thus offshore environments may be protected from pollution by the swamp separating them from the land. This is, of course, especially important where the land behind the swamp houses human communities, industry or agriculture.

Fig 4.5 *Mature stands of red mangrove can be an almost impenetrable tangle of prop roots.*

Fig 4.6 *The roots of black mangrove produce upward growing pneumatophores that enable the plant to take up oxygen for the roots despite the waterlogged soil.*

Fig 4.7 *In swamps with a big tidal range the pneumatophores need to be long so that at least the tops are above the water at all times. This picture was taken at about low tide in the Caroni Swamp in Trinidad.*

Black mangrove

Behind the belt of red mangrove trees on slightly higher ground grows the black mangrove. Its roots are not always covered by water but stand in fairly solid and usually waterlogged soil. This presents the tree with problems of root aeration as such soils contain little oxygen. In order to cope the roots produce upward growths (pneumatophores) which protrude from the soil and stand upright in the air enabling them to 'breathe'. In swamps with a big tidal range, like the Caroni of Trinidad, these pneumatophores can grow to considerable heights above the soil so that even at high tide the tips will still be in the air. Mature black mangrove trees can grow up to 21 m (70 ft), and have a more upright shape than red mangroves. The leaves of black mangroves are fairly narrow and have more or less pointed tips. While the undersurface of these leaves is greyish and coated with fine hairs, the upper side is shiny green and often sprinkled with salt crystals. The reason for the presence of the salt is that when the tree takes up water from its saline soil the salt comes too; this salt is surplus to requirements for the tree and so is excreted as a solution via the leaves where it dries to form crystals. The flowers are small (about 12 mm, $\frac{1}{2}$ in, across), stalkless and clustered in groups. As with the red mangrove, the seeds germinate while still inside the fruit but in this case they are relatively insignificant.

Fig 4.8 *Flowers of black mangrove.*

Fig 4.9 *Mangroves live in salt-laden, often saturated soils and take up excess salt along with the water they require. The black mangrove seen here excretes this salt through the leaves. The salt crystals on the surface of the leaves are a characteristic feature of this mangrove species.*

White mangrove

This tree grows to about the same size as the red mangrove. Although it prefers drier ground than the black mangrove, it also often has pneumatophores (not usually so many or so large as those of the black mangrove). It can be distinguished from other mangroves by its leaves, which lack obvious veins, have rounded ends and a pair of glands on the reddish leaf stalk at the base of the leaf itself. It carries clusters of small white flowers that are followed by leathery and pear-shaped fruits (18 mm, $\frac{3}{4}$ in). Once again the seeds tend to germinate in the fruit and the young roots may break out even before the fruit is shed.

Fig 4.10 *Leaves and fruits of white mangrove.*

Grey mangrove or buttonwood

These grow at the landward side of the swamp and although they can survive in damp and salty soils they have neither prop roots nor pneumatophores. They can be distinguished from other mangroves by the fact that their leaves occur alternately on either side of the stems whereas those of the other mangroves are in pairs opposite each other. Furthermore, the leaves have small glands on the lower surface at the junctions of the veins and the midrib. These trees often carry fruit that looks rather like an unripe blackberry. These stay on the plant for months, becoming dry and brown. Buttonwoods will grow in a range of habitats other than swamps and plant breeders have created a range of forms for gardens. A silver-leaved version is widely used in planting schemes throughout the Caribbean and is particularly popular for hotel grounds.

What lives where?

Mangrove swamps are totally unlike the previous habitats that we have described although they have some features of both. A fully developed swamp will have damp or wet mud exposed at low tide on and in which live creatures not wholly different from those that inhabit sandy shores. The prop roots of red mangroves, permanently immersed in sea water, offer a place for animals and plants to attach to that is similar to the hard surfaces of rocky shores. However, added to this is the presence of the trees themselves giving a three-dimensional complexity both above and below ground as well as contributing to the nutrients available. As a result much of the life here is characteristic of mangroves and often not found in abundance elsewhere.

Fig 4.11 *Grey mangrove leaves can be distinguished from those of other mangrove species by the presence of glands on the underside where the veins join the midrib (as well as having a pair in the leaf stalk).*

Fig 4.12 *The fruits of grey mangrove are rather like unripe blackberries and stay on the plant almost all year round. This species of mangrove can tolerate dry conditions and is seen here growing behind a sandy beach along with coconut palms.*

In mud and soil

Crabs are common on the surface of the ground, scuttling back and forth. When pursued they usually escape either into burrows or up the stems and roots of the mangroves. The burrow dwellers are usually **fiddler crabs**. There are a number of species of these crabs in the Caribbean, all of them relatively small (12–25 mm ($\frac{1}{2}$–1 in) across the carapace). They share a characteristic which makes the males at least easy to identify to their genus (*Uca*), namely that one of the claws is very large while the other is much smaller. The female has two identical small claws (both of which are used for feeding). The male uses its smaller claw for feeding too. However, the other much enlarged one is primarily used for social signalling, being waved both to attract females and to discourage rival males. Each species has its own distinctive pattern of waving. Interactions between males are usually settled simply on the basis of size, the smaller animal backing down, but displays between males of similar size can result in fights. These usually involve the locking together of the rivals' larger claws followed by what amounts to a wrestling match; the stronger crab usually succeeds in overturning the weaker at which point the issue is declared settled and the loser departs. Although largely ritualistic, these encounters can occasionally result in injury. Because of its visual importance the major claw is often brightly coloured. Fiddler crabs are gregarious and often occur in huge numbers; they can be seen to feed by picking up tiny pieces of detritus from the surface of the mud. In West Indian mangrove swamps there are two common species – **Burger's** and the **Caribbean fiddler crabs**. They are difficult to tell apart in the field, especially the females, but the male Burger's has red on its large claw which also has tubercles on the inner side while the Caribbean has a light brown major claw bearing only fine granulation on the inner side.

Two other crabs are commonly found on the swamp floor or on the roots and branches of the mangroves. The **mud crab** is about 5 cm (2 in) across and

Fig 4.13 *This is a male fiddler crab and the greatly enlarged claw can be clearly seen. This claw is used only in display; feeding is performed by the much smaller left claw. Females have two small claws that are both used in food gathering.*

has slightly unequal claws the tips of which are black. This coloration spreads into the palm of the claw for the fixed finger and the movable finger of the larger claw has a white tooth near the base. The **mangrove crab** (*Goniopsus*) is related to the Sally Lightfoot and is coloured orange to red with red claws. Both the carapace and the legs are striped with fine lines of raised beads.

Fig 4.14 *In suitable conditions fiddler crab populations can be very large. They are seen here on the surface of the mud but when alarmed they will quickly disappear down burrows.*

Fig 4.15 *This shows both sides of a West Indian murex shell. These large (10 cm, 4 in, or more) gastropods sometimes feed on mangrove oysters.*

Fig 4.16 *The mangrove periwinkle is common, often seen clinging to roots or stems above water level.*

The **coffee-bean snail** is common on the mud and also clings to mangrove roots. This snail, unlike most of its seashore relatives that have gills, takes oxygen from the air via a small 'lung' which opens through a small hole in its side. Although it can survive for some time under water it must come to the surface to replenish the air in the 'lung'. This pulmonate snail is related to many of the temperate regions' land snails and slugs that employ the same method of breathing. Its shell is up to 18 mm ($\frac{3}{4}$ in) long, coloured dark brown with one or more pale transverse stripes. The **turret horn shell** is also common on the mud surface. About 12 mm ($\frac{1}{2}$ in) long, this many whorled spire-shaped shell can occur in very great numbers under favourable conditions. Where the surface is covered with shallow water you will sometimes see murex snails on the mud, occasionally the **apple murex** but more often the spiky **West Indian murex**. These predatory molluscs feed on the oysters which are found on the mangrove roots (see page 104).

Fig 4.17 *Tree crab is the name given to a number of species that are widespread in mangrove swamps. This is* Aratus pisonii, *identified by having a carapace that is broad at the front but quite narrow at the back and claws possessing coarse hairs and bristles.*

In and on the mangrove trees

The commonest animals that live on the trees above water level are yet more snails and crabs. As well as the coffee-bean snail mentioned above you will be likely to find the **mangrove periwinkle**. This is larger than most of the rocky shore winkles reaching to 3 cm (1.2 in) and the shell, mostly brown, has the most recent whorl paler than the upper ones and bearing fine spiral grooves.

There are two agile crabs that spend most of the daylight hours in the leafy canopy of the red mangroves, namely the **tree crab** (*Aretus*) and *Sesarma curacaoense*, two more relatives of the Sally Lightfoot. The tree crabs are difficult to see clearly, let alone catch. They are fast moving, tend always to move to be on the opposite side of a stem from the observer and in the last resort will hurl themselves into the water. Of the crabs living in mangroves, the tree crab has the most triangular carapace, being very broad between the eyes but narrowing considerably at the rear. Although variable in colour it is usually greenish with red legs. There are a number of *Sesarma* species but *S. curacaoense* is relatively small (12 mm, $\frac{1}{2}$ in, across) and the carapace is almost square.

The other inhabitants of the canopy are numerous species of bird but these will be covered in Chapter 6. Two other vertebrates that are often seen in the trees of the Caroni Swamp in Trinidad are the **two-toed sloth** and the **tree boa**. This island has a fauna unique among the Caribbean islands

Fig 4.18 *Tree boas sometimes sleep on branches overhanging the channels of Trinidad's Caroni Swamp.*

due to the fact that it has only recently been separated from the South American mainland and thus it has a very rich range of species much like that of Venezuela. The two-toed sloth can sometimes be seen suspended in the branches of the mangroves. These animals eat a very low energy diet of tree leaves and have adapted to this poor quality food by becoming extremely inactive, a characteristic seen also in the eucalyptus leaf-eating koala and the bamboo-munching giant panda. The tree boa may be seen coiled up in the branches. Although also to be found on other islands in the southern Lesser Antilles, the Caroni offers a good chance of seeing this snake in its natural habitat.

Fig 4.19 *This red mangrove root has been lifted almost clear of the water and its attached fauna can be seen. The bivalves attach nearest the water level while lower down there is a forest of hydroid colonies in which are sponges and tunicates. This zoned fauna develops on mangrove roots where the tidal range is small (this example is from Kingston Harbour, Jamaica). Where tides are bigger the fauna is dominated by animals that can survive periods out of water, in particular bivalves.*

Fig 4.20 *This pink sponge grows luxuriantly on red mangrove roots.*

Attached to mangrove roots

Red mangrove prop roots are often immersed in the water and as such make a very suitable site for attached animals to settle and grow. There are differences between those that will settle where the tidal range is large (as in Trinidad) and where the range is small (for example in Jamaica). The latter condition is the most stable and results in the richest growth. Unfortunately for non-divers these animals are difficult to examine without cutting and removing the root, a highly destructive strategy only to be used in cases of serious research. Something of them may be seen either from the surface or by snorkelling, but even then many of the animals belong to groups that require specialist knowledge to identify in any detail (sponges, tunicates and so on). Often roots hanging down into the water from higher branches may not be fixed into the mud and so can be gently lifted out of the water to reveal their attached fauna. Keep an eye out for the following:

- **Sponges** come in a range of colours although pink forms are common. As the sponge grows over the root it often forms finger-like growths at the end of which is a hole, visible to the naked eye. This is the route through which filtered water exits from the sponge. The detritus- and plankton-laden water has been previously drawn into the sponge through minute pores over the surface. The inside of the sponge is a mass of tiny channels, which eventually coalesce at the exit pore, and it is in these channels where small particles of food are captured and ingested. The water current through the sponge is driven by the beating of tiny hair-like processes on the cells of the sponge that line the channels.

- **Annelid worms,** commonly found on mangrove roots, are various sorts of tubeworms. These mostly belong to two groups, the sabellids and the serpulids, commonly called **fanworms**. They construct a tube that is attached at its base to the mangrove root and in which the body of the worm is housed. From the head of the worm come a great number of long tentacles that are extended from the tube to form an inverted cone. This catches food particles from the water which are passed back to the mouth. When disturbed this fan of tentacles is rapidly withdrawn into the tube.
- **Bivalve molluscs** are common, often the dominant settlers on roots. The best known is the **mangrove oyster**, a large (up to 15 cm, 6 in) bivalve with one smaller flat valve fitting into the other much more cupped one. This oyster is a commercial crop in many parts of the Caribbean and used to be harvested by the tonne in Caribbean countries with large swamps. There is now concern that its numbers may be diminishing in some locations and that perhaps it is being replaced by the less commercially useful **green mussel**. This mussel is an introduction from the Indian/Pacific Ocean region, and like many introduced species it has taken off throughout the Caribbean and the Gulf of Mexico and is now regarded by many as a pest species – a sort of molluscan weed. It first appeared outside of its native environment at Point Lisas in Trinidad in 1990 and was subsequently recorded in Venezuela in 1992 and Jamaica in 1998.

Fig 4.21 *The two valves on the left show an open Caribbean oyster; a closed specimen is shown bottom right. The two valves top right show the inside and the outside of a green mussel. The green rim to the valves is much more obvious in life.*

Fig 4.22 *Lister's tree oyster grows attached to a range of hard substrates, including mangrove roots. The hinge area has four to eight grooves on the inside.*

It has also been recorded in the Gulf of Mexico, establishing itself first in the estuarine habitats of west Florida such as Tampa Bay. The most likely route for this introduction is either by adult mussels arriving attached to the hulls of ships or by being transported as larvae in ballast water. Due to its rapid growth and high reproductive rates it is likely to spread within our region and to compete effectively against indigenous species.

Other oysters that are common on mangrove roots include the **flat tree oyster** and **Lister's tree oyster**. The former is more or less fan shaped and has eight to 12 close-set grooves inside the hinge whereas the latter is more elongate with only four to eight grooves inside the hinge. All of these bivalves flourish because of the rich suspended matter in the still waters of the swamp. However, their mode of feeding (by filtering the water) makes them susceptible to pollution effects. Oysters are often used as indicators of impurities in the water as some types of toxin are accumulated in the animals' tissues and so can be detected by analysis of the bivalves before the toxins are easily measured in the water. This bioamplification is useful in detecting, for example, increased levels of some harmful metals. Where there are oysters there will be drills and related snails that bore holes through the shells of the bivalves and eat the animal inside. The proboscis of these gastropods houses file-like mouthparts, the radula, and often also secretes acid which helps to dissolve the calcium carbonate shell of the oyster. These snails can reach nuisance levels where oysters are a commercial crop. The murexes have been mentioned above but the **Florida rock shell** is another that preys on oysters this way. It has a grey to yellow shell with darker mottlings and is smooth except for many fine spiral lines. Inside the opening is a strong ridge that runs back inside. It occurs not only in swamps but on rocky shores too.

- **Tunicates**, often called sea squirts, are important members of the mangrove root community. One of the commonest is the **black tunicate**. This has the appearance of an elongated sac up to 15 cm (6 in) long, black in colour, attached at one end and with two short tubes at the other, each ending with an obvious opening. If the root to which the animals are attached is taken out from the water and the animal touched or pressed it contracts, squirting water from the openings, hence the name. Inside the leathery sac is a large filter, actually a perforated part of the gut. Water is sucked in through one of the openings, passes through the filter, where food particles are removed, and is then pumped out through the second opening. The black tunicate, which is also often seen attached to harbour piles, is a solitary species but many tunicates are colonial. One colonial species is the **mangrove tunicate** often found covering lengths of mangrove root. Each individual has the typical sea squirt 'bag and two openings' structure but in this case they are only about 2.5 cm (1 in) long and transparent. The internal organs, in particular the gut, show through as pink, yellow or orange lines. The individuals are joined by root-like stolons at the bases. This colonial theme is taken further in the compound sea squirts in which individuality is lost. They usually appear as a thin gelatinous covering on hard surfaces. In the jelly are tiny star-shaped structures that represent a number of individuals arranged around the shared central siphon.

Living in the open water of the swamp

Most of the animals living in the channels and lagoons of mangrove swamps are outside the scope of this book, being visible only if one snorkels or dives. Even in shallow water most of the more mobile animals such as fish will take fright at the appearance of human observers. However, some of the slower and less shy can perhaps be seen. The **ragged sea hare** is sometimes to be found crawling over the mud in shallow lagoons. If disturbed it will emit clouds of purple dye, presumably as an anti-predator reaction. The **upside-down jellyfish**, also a common inhabitant of seagrass beds, is unmistakable. It is indeed a jellyfish but in the tentacles are symbiotic algae. These microscopic algae presumably contribute nutrition to the jellyfish in exchange for a protected environment. In order to maximise the light for the algal photosynthesis the jellyfish has adopted the eponymous upside-down position with its tentacles pointing skywards and the bell resting on the substrate. Big ones can be 30 cm (1 ft) across and are a spectacular sight.

One fish that can be seen in swamp channels is the **four-eye** fish. This intriguing animal swims with its head part way out of the water so that the upper half of the eye is above the surface while the lower half is below it. The structure of the two halves is slightly different to allow for the different optical properties of air and water so that the fish can see in both media.

Fig 4.23 *A ragged sea hare seen in a shallow lagoon. This creature produces clouds of purple fluid if disturbed.*

Fig 4.24 *The upside-down jellyfish also lives in shallow lagoons (see text).*

When approached, it will swim off at great speed, much of the body rising out of the water as the tail beats furiously – the nearest thing you'll see to an animal jet ski. These 15 cm (6 in) fish are often seen patrolling in pairs in the deeper tidal waters of the Caroni Swamp in Trinidad.

Fig 4.25 *The so-called American crocodile (not to be confused with the alligator) is a common sight during boat trips on the Black River of Jamaica.*

On the reptilian front, mention must be made of the Jamaican Black River crocodiles. This species (*Crocodilus acutus)* usually goes under the common name of the **American crocodile** and is not to be confused with the alligator of Florida and other southern states of the United States. The Black River has a rich mangrove swamp on its banks, known locally as The Morass. River trips can be taken to visit the mangrove habitat and one of the highlights is the likelihood of seeing American crocodiles. These are large reptiles with fully grown males typically reaching 5 m (16 ft) in length with recorded lengths of 7 m (22 ft). Despite their size and carnivorous diet there are very few authenticated cases of attacks on humans and the food seems to be mainly fish. Eggs are laid in a burrow or a nest of leafy debris and there is often parental protection of both the nest and the newly hatched offspring. In Trinidad and Tobago it is possible to see the **spectacled caiman**, a relative of the alligator. However, it seems less prepared to inhabit saline environments than the American crocodile preferring freshwater wetlands such as Trinidad's Nariva Swamp. It is a relatively small crocodilian with males and females reaching 2.5 m (8 ft) and 1.4 m (4.5 ft) respectively. As with the American crocodile, eggs are laid in a nest which is protected and there is parental care of the hatchlings by the females.

Another large predator in the swamps is man. As was mentioned earlier in this chapter, mangrove swamps are productive and act as nursery grounds for many animals which will spend their adult lives in the open sea. Some fish can spend their whole lives in the swamps and may reach considerable sizes while large predatory fish will enter the swamps from time to time to feed in these rich hunting grounds. Consequently the lagoons and channels in swamps can be very worthwhile fishing grounds. Because of the complexity of the swamps the fishing is not amenable to large commercial efforts thus swamps are more often exploited by individual fishermen using traditional methods.

Environmental importance of mangroves swamps

Mangrove swamps act as gigantic buffers between land and sea, protecting each from the other. The swamps occur in areas of flat land by the sea or in river estuaries, the very places most at risk during hurricanes. During such violent storms loss of life and property damage are particularly likely where wind-driven waves and sea water can invade the land. The presence of a mangrove-lined margin will do much to protect the inshore areas. Even at quieter times mangroves will reduce wave action and indeed turn land erosion into land creation through the capture of sediment among the roots. Conversely, the muddy environment of the swamp will protect the sea from a range of materials of land origin. Runoff and river-borne sediments will tend to accumulate in the swamp protecting offshore habitats such as coral reefs which are susceptible to damage from too much suspended material. Furthermore, the fine particles of the swamp mud, many of which are organic, have the ability to bind a range of chemicals including polluting metals. Thus many substances that might be toxic or able to encourage

Fig 4.26 *Even in fairly unlikely conditions red mangroves will attempt to establish themselves. Here they are struggling somewhat on the small offshore Jamaican island of Lime Cay.*

eutrophication will be retained within the swamp rather than be washed out into the sea. This is particularly important where there are human settlements behind the swamp as the mud particles will also trap and break down sewage materials. In financial terms it has been calculated that this filtering and purifying action can be valued at nearly US$1200 (£670) per year per hectare of swamp at 1998 prices. Similar calculations (published in *Intercoast Network*, Number 32, 1998) value mangrove fisheries at US$1578 and timber and charcoal production at US$1082 per year per hectare. When one adds the increasing interest in the natural history of mangroves and their potential for ecotourism, the case for their preservation, even restoration, seems obvious. None the less destruction in the name of 'progress' continues in many places.

5 Seashore Plants

This chapter is intended to be a guide to the commoner flowering trees, shrubs and herbs that grow on or close behind the seashore. It will not consider more primitive forms of plant life such as ferns, mosses or seaweeds. The very specialised trees that grow in mangrove swamps have been discussed in Chapter 4.

The seashore is not a fixed environment but is always changing. This is as a result of storms among other things, but also the more gradual processes of erosion and sedimentation. However, plants also contribute by colonising seashores and reducing erosion. Grasses and other low-growing plants colonise sandy beaches just above the tideline gradually turning the area into soil. They also capture wind-blown sand adding to and stabilising dunes which can then be colonised by shrubs and eventually trees. Other examples of this are mangrove swamps and other marshy plants. On rocky substrates, trees such as figs can exploit cracks and cause pieces to break off which will eventually form soil particles. During storms sandy beaches can get washed away but this is greatly reduced by the presence of trees such as coconut palms and manchineel (see Fig 7.10 on page 162).

Fig 5.1 *The plants in the foreground are growing on rocks at the top of a gully with very little soil. This results in a shortage of water and nutrients so the plants show xerophytic adaptations. These include leaves that may be small, rolled, hairy or waxy, all of which cut down water loss. These plants are often slow growing and may show 'sculpting' by the wind. Bottom Bay, Barbados. See also Fig 5.17 on page 124.*

For plants the characteristic feature of seashore environments is the scarcity of fresh water. This is because rainfall drains quickly through sand and off rocky surfaces; the often windy conditions cause rapid evaporation and salt, in the form of spray or sea water seeping through the sand, lowers the ability of plants to take up fresh water. This results in the same sort of conditions that desert plants have to contend with. Thus many of the same adaptations are seen in both groups of plants. Plants that can tolerate these conditions are called xerophytes. Leaves may be small, thick or waxy to cut down water loss and others have fine hairs that reduce heat absorption. Other adaptations to leaf shape include rolling or folding to reduce the surface from which water evaporates. Seaside plants are often woody and slow growing due to limited resources or they may be fleshy and succulent (able to store water in both stems and leaves) and quick growing and therefore able to take advantage of periodic rainfall. The plants' roots are often shallow and widespread to capture rainfall or they may have a single deep taproot. Those plants that live nearest to the shore have specially adapted roots that reject salt.

The effects of wind and salt

Many Caribbean islands, for example Barbados, have very different coastlines on the windward and the leeward sides. This is caused directly by the effects of wind itself, but also indirectly by the amount of salt in the atmosphere. On the windward side salt, in the form of spray or crystals, may

Fig 5.2 *The beach and sand dunes on the windward (east) coast of Barbados. Beach morning glory (Fig 5.5, page 115) and crab grasses are colonising the beach and aiding the capture of wind-blown sand to form dunes. Further up the dunes low-growing shrubs like sea grape (Fig 5.13, page 121) are becoming established.*

be blown a long way inland from the shore and thus influence the environment for plants. Plants on this shore are often either low growing or have quite obviously been 'sculpted' by the wind. They are also likely to be further from the water's edge. On the leeward or sheltered shores plants will be much nearer the water and are often large trees. In some islands these two types of vegetation are not strictly confined to windward or leeward sides of islands but are related to the amount of shelter or exposure generally.

At best, plants tolerate or cope with salt but most grow better the lower the salinity. The ability to tolerate levels of salt depends both on the type of plant and its adaptations and also on the water-holding capacity of the soil. This latter may vary within very short distances from the shore. As noted before, distance also controls the amount of salt in the air.

The plants found on Caribbean seashores may occur widely round the world in similar habitats. This is because they were either introduced from elsewhere and have now become naturalised or they arrived without the agency of man, for example the coconut. Other plants may be native to the region or in other cases closely related species have evolved in different islands. One well-known example of the latter is the agave or century plant. Finally there are endemic species that have only been found in one island but these would be rare except for the largest islands or the Caribbean mainland.

Fig 5.3 *A typical piece of natural sheltered or leeward shore in Tobago. Coconut palms are growing on the beach itself.*

Fig 5.4 *Century plant or maypole growing near Nelson's Dockyard in Antigua. It can grow on steep, rocky shores with little soil and its flower stalk takes many years to appear. However, it quickly lengthens up to 6 m (20 ft). Related species of this magnificent plant have evolved on different Caribbean islands.*

It is possible to divide seashore plants into four groups:

1. Those that tolerate the conditions nearest to the sea are usually low-growing grasses and other plants, often having long creeping stems. They can cope with a shifting substrate and other changes in conditions. They are often restricted to seashore habitats because they are unable to compete with other plants where the conditions are better.

2. The next group are mostly shrubby plants that can tolerate some salt and windy conditions.
3. Wind and salt-tolerant larger shrubs and trees that grow on more stable or sheltered areas of shoreline. These form a barrier to protect the natural forest that would have been the typical vegetation of Caribbean islands.
4. These plants, more typical of deserts, are found on rocky ground or other open situations where water shortage is most acute. The following are examples of the more common or noticeable plants from these four groups.

Low-growing plants

One of the most conspicuous plants in this group is the **beach morning glory** also known as the seaside yam, sea vine or goat's-foot ipomoea. It has long, strong purplish stems that creep out over the sand with fleshy round leaves that are notched at the tip. The flowers are usually borne singly, funnel shaped, mauve, with a deeper colour in the middle and are about 5 cm (2 in) across. Beach morning glory is one of the first plants to colonise sandy shores, as it can cope with blown sand found widely on tropical shores.

Fig 5.5 *Beach morning glory is one of the very early colonisers on sandy shores and can also be found on flat rocky surfaces with little soil. It has long purplish stems and single trumpet-shaped mauve flowers. With its tough shiny green, somewhat succulent leaves it can cope with blown sand.*

Stings from marine animals may be eased by applying young morning glory leaves as they apparently have antihistamine properties.

There are two creeping grasses that commonly colonise sandy shores with morning glory (see Fig 5.2 on page 112). They are called **crab grass** and **beach knot grass** (and may both confusingly be called crab grasses). They are difficult to tell apart unless they are flowering. Crab grass has a predominantly single flower stalk (inflorescence) while the flowers of beach knot grass are on a forked spike. They both have long creeping rhizomes (underground stems) and stolons (creeping stems above ground). Both species are found widely on Old and New World warm seashores.

Another creeping plant that looks like beach morning glory at first glance is the **sea bean** or horse bean. This is a member of the pea family with inflorescences of pinkish purple pea-like flowers growing out of the leaf axils along the stems. The leaves are divided into three rounded leaflets and it has flattened pods up to 15 cm (6 in) long. The sea bean can grow quite far down beaches but is also found in disturbed ground such as roadsides. The seeds are poisonous if eaten raw and the dried beans are dangerously hallucinogenic.

Fig 5.6 *The sea bean grows further away from the water's edge than beach morning glory which it superficially resembles. The leaves consist of three rounded leaflets and the pinkish purple pea-like flowers grow in inflorescences from the leaf axils. The flattened pods and seeds are dangerous if eaten.*

Fig 5.7 *This spreading little plant, seaside samphire, grows at the back of beaches in stable situations and on rocky shores. It has very fleshy cigar-shaped leaves and reddish stems. The little flowers are star shaped and pink. The leaves can make a salty addition to salads and used to be eaten to treat scurvy.*

Seaside samphire or sea purslane is another low-growing plant which has spreading reddish stems and small very fleshy, cigar-shaped leaves. Its pink star-like little flowers are carried singly. This plant grows further up the beach in more stable soil or on cliffs and rocky shores. The leaves can be used in salad to provide a salty addition and formerly were eaten to treat scurvy. Seaside samphire occurs worldwide in the tropics and sub-tropics. **Red wild purslane** can easily be confused with seaside samphire but it has longer, less swollen leaves.

Another plant known as **samphire** or salt weed is a fleshy spreading plant with rounded heads of tiny white or straw-coloured flowers. The leaves are small, cylindrical and very succulent. The shoots can be cooked and eaten. Samphire grows on rocks near the sea and on sandy shores above the high tide mark as well as on muddy banks in mangrove swamps. It occurs in the Caribbean islands and also in continental tropical America and Florida.

Fig 5.8 *Samphire or salt weed is a fleshy, spreading plant with very succulent cylindrical leaves and tiny white or straw-coloured flowers in round heads. It is growing just behind the colonising crab grasses as it needs slightly more stable sandy shores, but it also grows on rocks near the sea as well as on muddy banks in swamps. The shoots are edible when cooked. Pigeon Point, Tobago.*

Fig 5.9 *Purslane is a low spreading plant when it occurs on rocky or other seaside habitats. It also occurs as a weed elsewhere and then it is much more upright. Its small cup-shaped yellow flowers are only open in the morning. It has long been eaten, either cooked rather like spinach or raw in salads.*

Purslane, also known as pussley or hog meat, is a very variable low-growing herbaceous plant whose appearance depends on the conditions in which it is growing. On rocky shores and other seaside places it is flat and spreading with little fleshy leaves and small cup-shaped yellow flowers that are only open in the mornings. Where it occurs as a garden weed it is upright to 40 cm (16 in) high. It occurs worldwide in suitable latitudes and has a long history in the kitchen, being used in salads and callaloo (a dish like cooked spinach, a part of some traditional West Indian breakfasts). It is also used as a poultice for swellings and sprains in both the Caribbean and Ghana.

Seaside daisy has white daisy flowers with yellow centres. Its spreading stems put down roots irregularly into the sand.

Two herbaceous plants that grow behind the beach which do not have such an obviously creeping habit and have quite showy flowers are the **carpet daisy** (also known as marigold or pissweed) and the **periwinkle** (old maid's bush or Cayenne jasmine). The carpet daisy does have creeping stems but the flowers are on upright stems. It has showy yellow flowers and occurs in the Caribbean and central regions of the Americas. The periwinkle is originally from Madagascar and is often planted but also occurs widely in waste places such as behind beaches. It stands about 60 cm (2 ft) high and has rose pink or red and white flowers. The periwinkle is the origin of the vinca alkaloids, an important group of anti-cancer drugs. Finally, **small seaside lavender** is a common plant of damp hollows among rocks and in swampy areas as well as behind beaches, with a very characteristic curved, forked inflorescence of small white flowers. The leaves are grey-green and fleshy.

Fig 5.10 *Seaside daisy has white flowers with yellow centres and the stems put down roots into the sand along their length which helps to anchor the plant in such a shifting substrate.*

Fig 5.11 *The periwinkle is originally from Madagascar but is now found often behind beaches as well as being grown as a garden plant. The flowers come in a range of colours from white through pink to red and may also be pink with a darker red centre. This plant is well known in medicine, being the origin of the vinca alkaloids which are important anti-cancer drugs. English Harbour, Antigua.*

Fig 5.12 *Small seaside lavender is a common seaside plant in a range of different situations. It has a very characteristic curved and forked inflorescence of tiny white flowers.*

Shrubs

On windward or exposed shores the shrubby zone at the back of the beach proper is often 'sculpted' by the wind on the sea side where there may be a considerable amount of damaged, leafless branches. On rocky shores the shrubs occur at the top of the cliff or in gullies down to the sea. The chief characteristic of these habitats is lack of water so many of the plants have xerophytic adaptations.

One of the main plants in these habitats is the **sea grape** which can form very dense stands of bushes. It should also be noted that on more sheltered shores the sea grape can grow to a sizeable tree and is often quite close to the water's edge as its fruits float and are salt tolerant. It has large leathery and shiny leaves like saucers that are reddish when young. The small greenish cream flowers are in spikes 15–30 cm (6–12 in) long which produce fruit that look like clusters of grapes, green when young but turning reddish purple later.

Fig 5.13 *The sea grape is a very common seaside shrub or in sheltered conditions a sizeable tree. It is often found very close to the water's edge, one reason being that its fruits float and are salt tolerant. It has round glossy leaves and spikes of tiny white flowers. These develop into hanging clusters of grape-like fruit, green when unripe, as here, but turning purplish later.*

Fig 5.14 *Seaside mahoe may be a shrub or a tree. It is also called hibiscus tree, tulip tree or catalpa because of the shape of its leaves (heart shaped) and flowers. The flowers are pale yellow with dark centres and as they age they turn pink or purple. Kingston Harbour, Jamaica.*

Another plant that may be a shrub or a tree depending on its situation is the **seaside mahoe** also called hibiscus tree, tulip tree or catalpa. This has heart-shaped leaves and striking pale yellow flowers with dark centres. As the flowers age they turn pink or purple. It grows on a variety of shores and can be found very near the water. It has hard wood that is resistant to termites and so is used in boat and other building. The flowers are edible and the leaves apparently have medicinal uses. **Bay cedar** is often a branched shrub but can grow to 8 m (27 ft). It has small hairy, yellow-green leaves and small yellow flowers. It is found on beaches and sand dunes.

Sweet briar in the acacia family is a shrub that has fierce long spines and pinnate leaves. The flowers are in spherical heads and are bright yellow and scented. It has cylindrical green pods up to 15 cm (6 in) long and it occurs in the West Indies and Central America.

Other shrubs have small, often greyish leaves and are not particularly noteworthy unless they are in flower. They include **rock** or **white sage** with small hairy twigs and leaves and heads of small pink flowers and little round purplish fruits. Both can be seen on the plant at the same time as they flower at any time of the year following rain. **Strumpfia** (also called false rosemary) is a low-growing shrub of rocky sea cliffs and sand dunes. It has small narrow leaves that are woolly underneath and little pink or white flowers and round white fruits. **Seaside sage** or yellow balsam is a common shrub in dry rocky

Fig 5.15 *Bay cedar has a typically xerophytic habit with small hairy, fleshy and densely packed leaves. It is often a small shrub but can grow to 8 m (27 ft). It has small yellow flowers and flourishes in dry situations on beaches, sand dunes and rocky shores. Tortola, British Virgin Islands.*

Fig 5.16 *Sweet briar, in the acacia family, has fierce long spines and finely cut leaves. The bright yellow scented flowers are in dense heads like little balls. It has green pods up to 15 cm (6 in) long.*

sites near the sea. It has grey-green pointed leaves and spikes of small white flowers which are fragrant. **Fat pork** or cocoplum is a shrub of sand dunes and other sandy soil. It has round leathery leaves and inconspicuous flowers. The round purple-red fruits are astringent but edible and are eaten raw or made into jam or jelly.

Fig 5.17 *Seaside sage or yellow balsam is a xerophytic shrub with greyish woolly leaves that grows in very dry situations on rocky cliffs or gullies. It is slow growing and has small fragrant white flowers.*

Seashore trees

A fringe of trees is an integral part of the view of the idyllic tropical beach. In the Caribbean this is true of most beaches that are reasonably sheltered. In some cases the trees will have been largely planted to further the cause of tourism but in other cases the vegetation is entirely natural.

Coconut palms may be thought of as the most typical tree to fringe a beach and it is probably also the most widely useful tree in the world (see Fig 5.3, page 113). Different communities around the world use all parts of this tree in one way or another. Additionally, there are commercially important uses such as coconut oil, coir for rope, padding, etc., and synthetic rubber. Coconuts are not restricted to seashores, being planted commercially in many tropical countries. However, one of the reasons that they are found so widely on beaches is the ability of the nuts to float and survive long periods in sea water and when washed up on a beach to germinate and flourish. As noted earlier their roots may help to prevent sand being washed away during storms.

Fig 5.18 *Coconut palms occur on beaches around the tropical world as the nuts float and can be washed up on to beaches where they germinate. You can see them at all stages of growth on and behind sheltered beaches. See also Fig 5.3 on page 113.*

Another tree that was not originally native to the region but has been absorbed into the local flora is the **seaside almond** (also called the Barbados or Indian almond) which originated in India. The tree grows to 9 m (30 ft) with horizontal branches and rounded leaves that turn red before they fall. The flowers are in spikes, mainly male but with a few hermaphrodite (male and female) flowers near the base. These develop into green, almond-shaped fruit about 6 cm (2 in) long. Both the outer coat and the nut inside are edible. The outside of the fruit has a corky layer making them buoyant like coconuts. The leaves and bark contain tannin and in India they are mixed with iron salts to make Indian ink. They are also used to make medicinal 'teas' for a range of ills.

Fig 5.19 *A native of India, the seaside almond is a very common beachside tree. It has rounded leaves that turn red before they fall off. The flowers occur in spikes, mainly male but with a few hermaphrodite ones near the base. These form almond-shaped, edible green fruit. The outer layer is corky making them buoyant like coconuts.*

Fig 5.20 *The almonds of seaside almond are frequently found on beaches in all states of decay.*

A local tree that is often found near beaches but also in dry rocky inland areas is **manchineel** also known as beach or poison apple. These latter names derive from the small yellow-green 'apples' that are poisonous and indeed fatal if eaten in quantity. The other concern with manchineels is that their caustic sap can cause blistering on the skin and even blindness, so in many islands these trees have been removed from tourist beaches. In other places, including Barbados, each tree is marked in red and there are notices warning of the dangers, including not sheltering under them during rain (see Fig 8.2 on page 168). Figure 7.10 on page 162 shows the effect of wave erosion round manchineel roots.

Another tree that has been widely planted on seashores as a shade tree and to stabilise beaches is **casuarina** or mile tree or Australian beefwood, an Australian native that looks rather like a conifer. It is now more or less naturalised. Casuarinas show extreme xerophytic adaptation as the 'leaves' are actually green branches and the leaves proper are reduced to tiny scales. The fruits look like very small, round fir cones and are often seen in large numbers on beaches. The tree forms a very effective wind break so is also planted along roadsides.

Fig 5.21 *Manchineel trees, also known as beach or poison apple trees, are beachside trees often growing only just above the high tideline. When the beach profile changes, for example after a storm or after nearshore reef destruction, the roots become exposed (see Fig 7.10, page 162). The small yellow-green 'apples' (inset) are poisonous and the sap from the whole plant is caustic and causes skin blisters and even blindness. For this reason manchineels have been removed from tourist beaches in many islands. Elsewhere, as in Barbados, there are notices warning of the dangers (see Fig 8.2 on page 168).*

Fig 5.22 *An Australian native tree, the casuarina is often planted behind beaches both to help stabilise them and to provide shade. Superficially looking like a conifer, it is in fact an extreme zerophyte with the leaves reduced to tiny scales on green branches. The fruits look like small round fir cones and are found in large numbers on beaches under the trees. In front is a scarlet cordia.*

A native tree of the West Indies is **scarlet cordia** (or geranium tree, geiger tree or anaconda), which is often planted in gardens but also grows wild or planted along beaches. It has showy bunches of orange-scarlet flowers on a smallish tree. The fruits have a roundish white fleshy coating and may be found along beaches.

Fig 5.23 *The scarlet cordia is a native West Indian tree that grows wild or is planted behind beaches as well as being used in gardens. It is also known as the geranium tree and has attractive bunches of orange-scarlet flowers. The fruits are round with a whitish fleshy coat and can be found on the beach.*

Fig 5.24 *Barringtonia is often planted by the sea as in this case beside St George's Harbour in Grenada. Like many other seaside trees the large grey heart-shaped fruits are buoyant and can be distributed by the sea (inset). The tree has sizeable glossy leaves and the large pale flowers have very showy pink and white stamens. These are mostly found on the ground in the morning because they open in the evening and only last one night.*

A less common seaside tree is **barringtonia** that comes from Asia. As with many other seaside trees its large, grey and heart-shaped fruits are buoyant and distributed by water. The leaves are large and the flowers cluster at the ends of the branches. The big flowers, with showy pink and white stamens, open only in the evening. These are shed during the night and can be seen under the tree the following morning. The seeds from distinctive shaped fruits can be grated and used by fishermen to stun fish.

The **shortleaf** or **bearded fig** is a tree that grows on cliffs, using cracks to get a foothold. It may be very bent and shaped by the wind. As well as the normal roots, others grow directly from the branches giving a beard-like appearance, hence the name. These roots can be very long and may reach the beach below. The plant can also grow as an epiphyte on another tree and eventually smother it. It has leathery, shiny leaves and the figs are round and yellow when ripe.

Fig 5.25 *The shortleaf or bearded fig grows on cliffs getting a foothold using cracks and then sending down roots, sometimes right down to the shore below. Roots come from the branches as well as the base of the plant forming the 'beard'. It has leathery leaves and small round figs that are yellow when ripe.*

Fig 5.26 *The tamarind is a common large shade tree that is wind, salt and drought tolerant. Its most noticeable feature is the knobbly brown seedpods containing several shiny squarish seeds. These are surrounded by a sweet but astringent pulp that is used, mixed with sugar, to make confectionery bars as well as jam.*

A seashore tree from the same family as seaside mahoe is the **sea hibiscus**. It is a spreading tree or large shrub which has branches that can root into the sand. The yellow flowers are short lived, some with dark red centres; they turn orange later in the day.

The **tamarind** is a large tree naturalised (probably from Africa) but also planted. It makes a very wind-, salt- and drought-tolerant shade tree. The flowers are yellowish but the more noticeable feature is the brown knobbly pods. They have squarish seeds inside surrounded by a sweet but astringent pulp. The latter has had medicinal uses since antiquity but in the West Indies it is now used to make a confectionary bar when mixed with sugar. It is also made into jam and used in other ways in the kitchen. The wood is hard and difficult to work but makes handsome furniture.

Finally, it should be noted that **seaside mahoe** and **sea grape** have been described above in the Shrubs section but given the right conditions they can grow into large seaside trees.

Desert-like plants

Perhaps the most striking of plants in this group is the **century plant** or maypole (a member of the agave family) which flourishes on steep, rocky slopes with little soil (see Fig 5.4 on page 114). Closely related species occur in different islands. It has a rosette of wax-coated spear-like leaves with very sharp blackish spines at the tips. The name derives from the fact that the flower stalk takes many years (but not a century!) to appear although once it does it grows very rapidly. The bright yellow flowers are arranged in clusters up the stem which may be up to 6 m (20 ft) tall and very imposing. The flower stalks are used as floats by fishermen and were previously used for rafts. Other plants with a similar habit that may also be seen are **yucca**, a Central American native with white flowers, and **aloe**. The latter is originally from the Mediterranean coast but has been introduced and is now widely naturalised.

Fig 5.27 *The candelabra or columnar cactus is an unbranched plant that often grows in clumps as here in Antigua. It is very slow growing, but may reach 5 m (16 ft) and plants may be as much as 100 years old. From August to October they produce single white flowers on the spiny, ridged round stems. The round red fruit are edible.*

There are three cacti commonly seen on or near Caribbean seashores. The most spectacular is the **columnar** or **candelabra cactus**, also known as the pipe organ or dildo cactus. This grows very slowly, up to 5 m (16 ft) high and may be as much as 100 years old. It is unbranched but often grows in large groups. The stems are round with many needle-like spines along ridges.

Fig 5.28 *On open, dry wasteland near the sea you can find turks cap cactus. This is barrel shaped and covered with spines. Note the woolly and bristly structure on top called a cephalium from which bright pink flowers will emerge. These are followed by edible pink fruit that are sweet and juicy. Nelson's Dockyard, Antigua.*

Fig 5.29 *A cactus well known from other parts of the world is opuntia or prickly pear – locally known as flat-hand dildo. It can be found on dry seashore land and has yellow or orange flowers followed by dark red pear-shaped edible fruit.*

Single white flowers appear near the tops of branches from August to October, followed by round red fruits which are edible. The **turks cap cactus** is a short, barrel-shaped plant that is seen on dry, open scrubby situations near the sea. It develops a vertical woolly and bristly structure (cephalium) on top, up to 30 cm (1 ft) high, from which bright pink flowers emerge between the bristles. The fruits are also bright pink and edible, being sweet and juicy. Finally, the well-known **prickly pear** or opuntia (locally known as flat-hand dildo) occurs on dry seashore land. It grows to 2 m ($6\frac{1}{2}$ ft) and has yellow or orange flowers followed by dark red pear-shaped fruit. The latter are edible and the pads are used to make medicinal 'teas'.

6 Seashore Birds

Books on shore life tend to omit any mention of birds. There are a number of reasons for this that may include one or more of the following:

1. The authors of seashore guides are usually marine biologists with relatively little knowledge of ornithology.
2. Bird studies have a very strong amateur following and the field is well supported by readily available books and magazines.
3. Although birds are important members of the coastal ecosystems they tend to fly away when the beachcomber approaches and 'out of sight' often means 'out of mind' for those writing about the biology of seashores.

This short chapter gives some basic information on the commoner members of the seaside avifauna. Those wanting more detail are referred to the excellent books devoted solely to Caribbean ornithology (see Bibliography on page 177).

Fig 6.1 *The Brown booby (*Sula leucogaster*) has a distinctive silhouette in which the wings seem to be set quite far back on the body of the bird.*

Place of birds in beach ecosystems

A number of birds that can be seen from beaches or in mangrove swamps feed in deep waters and only use the land for roosting or nesting. These include the tropicbirds, boobies and frigatebirds all of which tend to fish in deep water either by plunge diving (the first two) or by picking up fish close to the surface (the last). Frigatebirds will also pursue and harass smaller sea birds in the hope of persuading them to disgorge or drop their catch. The brown pelican fishes nearer inshore, sometimes diving headlong into water so shallow that one fears for its safety. The terns also feed by diving for fish often far out to sea although the royal tern tends to hunt nearer the shore. The waders mostly feed on the beach, sometimes chasing down the sand after retreating waves to capture tiny invertebrates (sanderlings), sometimes searching for similar prey among pebbles and washed-up seaweed (turnstones) or attacking bivalves attached to rocks (American oystercatcher).

Many of the birds seen on beaches will not be committed to seaside life, simply using the shore as just one of the habitats in which they spend time. The herons and egrets will probably be exploiting a range of wetland and other inland sites and the grackles, bullfinches and vultures are essentially land birds that may on occasions exploit beaches (and often scrounge from the human occupants). No matter in what way birds exploit the seashore, there is no doubt that they can, collectively, make a considerable impact on the ecosystem. Having said that, it must be realised that some birds only come ashore to roost or nest while others may briefly visit on autumn or spring migration so that their influence might be slight or transitory. There is also little doubt that many are vulnerable to the changes that Man is making in the Caribbean. In particular those that are confined to nesting only at particular sites are at risk if these places are disturbed by human activity.

Birds commonly seen on or from shores

Tropicbirds are elegant tern-like birds, largely white in colour and (in adults) having two long tail feathers called streamers. There are two species in the Caribbean, the **red-billed** and the **white-tailed,** which are not easy to distinguish. The former has narrow black barring on the back and wings, a stout red bill and black eye stripes which may meet on the nape of the neck. The latter lacks barring but has a single heavy black band in its place, the bill is yellow or orange and the eye stripes are never long enough to meet on the neck. They both breed in small numbers on the sea cliffs of a number of islands and are most likely to be seen close to their nesting sites in early morning. One such nesting area is on Little Tobago and boat trips can be organised from Speyside to see them.

Of the boobies found in the Caribbean the one most frequently seen is the **brown booby**. This bird is related to the European gannet and has a similar outline with long pointed wings and a head and neck that extend much further forward of the wings than those of gulls. The adult brown booby is dark above but with a white lower breast, belly and underwings; the immature is entirely brown. They breed at various sites throughout the Caribbean and range widely. As mentioned above they feed by plunge diving sometimes from a considerable height and are also said to pursue flying fish when they leave the water.

Fig 6.2 *The flight silhouette of the brown pelican is unmistakable.*

Fig 6.3 *An adult brown pelican.*

The **brown pelican** is a familiar sight at many Caribbean beaches. This large bird is easy to identify as it flies by, often parallel to the shore, or when it perches on posts or pilings. It is mostly dark brown below and silvery grey above with a neck and head which are white in the winter and a rich brown in the summer except for the white face and throat. The bird has a long neck but in flight this is folded back to the shoulders giving a rather hunched appearance. Immature birds are brown above with paler underparts. The bill is extraordinary, being large and with a hugely extensible pouch on the lower mandible and throat. When feeding, the bird will often make multiple passes over the same area, diving with folded wings when fish are spotted. As the bird surfaces after a dive the catch can often be seen outlined inside the great pouch but it is soon swallowed, frequently with an exaggerated head toss. Brown pelicans are ground nesters and there are breeding colonies in various places throughout the region. As with many other Caribbean seabirds there is concern about diminishing numbers.

Another bird commonly seen flying near shores is the **magnificent frigatebird**. The outline of this bird against the tropical blue sky is an unmistakable and evocative sight. The wings are long and narrow with a bend at the 'wrist' while the longish tail is sometimes spread to reveal its forked shape. At a distance the birds look black but closer inspection shows

Fig 6.4 *A group of magnificent frigatebirds roosting in mangroves. The males have red chests and the females white chests. The insert shows the typical flight silhouette.*

that males have a red or orange throat patch (which can be inflated in courtship displays) while females have a white breast. The beak is long, thin and hooked. There is something about the shape and demeanour of these birds that suggests a piratical nature and this is not just an illusion as much of their food is obtained by bullying other smaller seabirds into dropping or regurgitating their recently caught prey. They will also swoop down to the sea surface to scoop up fish and are sometimes seen near fishing boats taking fish offal and waste thrown overboard. They nest in colonies throughout the region, usually on small offshore islands in bushes or trees.

A number of herons may spend part of their time on beaches or in mangrove swamps as well as seeking food in freshwater wetlands. The three that we have seen most often near the sea are the **green-backed heron**, the **little blue heron** and the **yellow-crowned night heron**. The first of these has, as its name indicates, a greyish back strongly tinged with green while the underparts are a beautiful dark chestnut colour. The bill is heavy with

Fig 6.5 *A little blue heron stalking prey in the shallows.*

some yellow on the lower mandible and a white stripe stretches from the throat down to the breast. On occasions this bird can be very tame and we have seen it scavenging around local beach-side fish markets in Tobago. The little blue heron is a more slender bird, coloured slate grey but with some hints of brown on the head and neck. The bill is paler at the base and black at the tip. Once more, as with the others of this trio, it can be encountered in a range of habitats but these include brackish swamps. Like the previous species they seem relatively unafraid of people and can often be approached quite closely. The yellow-crowned night heron is distinguished by its relatively squat shape, the very heavy dark bill and the bold face pattern of mainly black and white. Despite its name the crown is most often white or perhaps a light brown. The rest of the body is grey streaked with black while the legs are a distinctive yellow. The name is also misleading in that these birds are not wholly nocturnal and are often seen during the day, although most often close to dawn and dusk. They would seem to be creatures of habit and we have seen one individual that stalked the same section of sandy beach at the same time (early morning) every day for weeks. All these herons are fairly small with the maximum length of the green-backed reaching 48 cm (19 in) and the other two being 71 cm (28 in). As with other herons, they all fold the neck when flying.

Fig 6.6 *A yellow-crowned night heron on the beach at Castara Bay, Tobago.*

Fig 6.7 *Cattle egrets sometimes gather together in large numbers in mangroves either to nest or simply to roost. Their yellow and red bills and their yellow legs distinguish them from other egrets.*

Egrets are also members of the heron family. Some of the Caribbean egrets frequent beaches and because they often nest in mangroves they can sometimes be seen there too. The three species most likely to be seen are all white in general plumage. The **cattle egret** has a yellow bill and yellow-green legs; during the breeding season there are patches of golden plumage on the head, neck and back. This is a bird of Old World origins that has been expanding its range in recent decades. It first appeared in the Caribbean in the 1950s and is now common throughout the region. Most often it is seen in association with cattle, feeding on insects and other small animals disturbed by the bovine hooves, but it both nests and feeds in mangroves. The **common egret** is a larger bird (to 107 cm, 42 in, as compared with 64 cm, 25 in, for the cattle egret) and has much darker legs than the former. This elegant bird boasts splendid plumes on the upper breast and the base of the neck (and also on the shoulders during the breeding season). The immature is similar but lacks the plumes. It feeds on fish and aquatic invertebrates which it catches by standing motionless in shallow water until the unwary prey swims by. The **snowy egret** is much the same size as the cattle egret but has a black bill and black legs with yellow toes. Like the common egret it possesses long plumes from head, back and breast and was once exploited so that these could be used to decorate ladies' hats and so on. This trade has long been banned and numbers are recovering. This egret also hunts in shallow water but unlike the common egret it moves about actively in search of prey. All of these egrets breed in various places in the region but the cattle egret seems to be ubiquitous and common, sometimes having breeding colonies of thousands of birds.

Fig 6.8 *Scarlet ibis feeding in the Caroni Swamp, Trinidad.*

Mention must be made of the **scarlet ibis**. This is not in truth a Caribbean-wide bird as it is only to be seen commonly in Trinidad (although there are a small number in Tobago and a few vagrants have been reported in Grenada and one or two other islands). If the opportunity arises to visit Trinidad's Caroni Swamp, accept it if only to see these remarkable birds. The sight of these astonishingly bright red birds feeding on the mud flats or flying in at dusk to roost in the mangroves is unforgettable.

There are a number of waders commonly seen in the Caribbean, mostly on sandy shores but also on rocks. While some will be resident breeding species, many will be on migration and thus more likely to be observed in spring and autumn. We will cover a few of the species most likely to be seen but as the possibilities are fairly numerous it might be necessary to consult a more comprehensive ornithological guide. The **semipalmated plover** will be familiar to visitors from Europe, as it is a close relative of the ringed plover. This small bird (to 19 cm, 8 in) is grey-brown above and white beneath. Around the upper breast and encircling the neck is a black band. The top of the head is the same colour as the back except for the forehead which is black with a white patch immediately above the dark bill with its yellow base. This bird breeds in Arctic North America and so is usually seen on passage;

some non-breeding individuals are in the region all year round. The **American oystercatcher**, in contrast, is a resident breeding in the Greater Antilles and occurring also in other parts of the northern Caribbean. It is black or very dark brown except for white patches on the wings and rump and a white breast and underparts. It has a long, straight and bright red bill which is used to prise open molluscs such as mussels.

Fig 6.9 *The semipalmated plover often feeds just at the water's edge on sandy beaches.*

Fig 6.10 *Sanderlings breed up near the Arctic Circle but winter south as far as South America. Some winter in the Caribbean while others pass through in spring and autumn. A few non-breeders can even be seen in the summer.*

The **spotted sandpiper** is a commonly seen small wader on sandy beaches. In appearance it is fairly nondescript having brown upperparts and white below as far forward as the breast. The white also extends to a small patch on the shoulder just in front of the wing. The white underparts are finely spotted with black in the breeding season and it is this feature that gives the bird its name. However, in the Caribbean the birds are usually on migration and thus in winter plumage which lacks the spots. These sandpipers, which are usually solitary, have a very characteristic bobbing gait as they scour the wet sand for small invertebrates. The **sanderling** is another migrant wader seen on this type of beach. They are relatively easy to identify due to the overall pale appearance of their winter plumage (they breed much further north). More gregarious than spotted sandpipers, small groups of these busy birds often feed by chasing out over the sand after retreating waves, presumably taking advantage of the disturbed sand. The next breaker sends them scurrying up the beach again. **Turnstones** are another winter visitor (although non-breeders may stay in the Caribbean throughout the year). This solidly built wader is quite dark brown above and on most of the head and breast, white below and has orange legs. The underparts are a contrasting clear white and there are some paler patches on the neck and throat. In flight they show a complex pattern of dark brown with white on the base of the tail, down the back, at the wing bases and as a mid-wing bar. These birds feed, as their name suggests, by turning things over (sometimes stones but more usually seaweed and other debris on the beach) and catching the small animals thus revealed.

Visitors from more temperate regions may well be surprised by the relative lack of gulls in Caribbean waters, both in terms of simple numbers and the variety of species. The one species that is seen frequently throughout the region is the **laughing gull**. In breeding plumage this bird has a black head with the colour continuing quite a long way down the neck and a slate

Fig 6.11 *Turnstones, like sanderlings, are mainly winter visitors and passage migrants which breed in the far north.*

grey back. In winter plumage the head is basically white with some grey on the top and face. Like many other gulls it is catholic in its diet, taking fish from the sea, scavenging along the beach or feasting on offal at the fish markets. There is a greater variety of terns than of gulls in the Caribbean with the **royal tern** in particular being a relatively common sighting. This is a fairly big (to 50 cm, 20 in) and powerfully built tern with a heavy orange or yellow bill. The plumage is mostly white except for the grey back and the black cap on the head, elongated behind into a short crest. The tail is moderately forked. Another common species is the **bridled tern**. Smaller than the royal (to about 38 cm, 15 in) it is an altogether more lightly built bird. The back, wings and tail are a brownish grey and the black cap is broken by white running from the forehead to above and behind the eye. The very similar **sooty tern** has darker, almost black, upperparts merging at the back of the neck with the cap. The white patch on the forehead is smaller than that of the bridled and extends no further back than the eye. It nests in various places in the Caribbean, sometimes in colonies numbering tens of thousands of pairs. Unfortunately these colonies are raided by egg collectors as the eggs are thought to have aphrodisiac properties. The **sandwich tern** also breeds in the Caribbean and can be distinguished by the fact that its bill is black with a yellow tip.

As well as the true sea or seashore birds there are a number of more terrestrial species that have become adapted to exploit beaches especially where there are people. These include the grackles, the **Greater Antillean**

Fig 6.12 *Laughing gulls in breeding plumage gather on a beach close to a fish market.*

Fig 6.13 *A mixed group of royal terns (larger) with bridled terns (smaller) in Kingston Harbour, Jamaica.*

Fig 6.14 *Greater Antillean grackles acting as aggressive beggars in Jamaica.*

grackle and the **carib grackle** of the Lesser Antilles. The males of both of these are glossy black birds with contrasting white irises to the eyes while the females are duller, browner birds. In many tourist areas these birds have become beach pirates, quite aggressively snatching food from picnickers. At beachside tables both the various species of **bullfinch** and the **banana quit** will raid sugar bowls and jam dishes. Another unlikely exploiter of beaches is the **black vulture** which in Trinidad (the only Caribbean island where this species is common) is often seen scavenging dead fish.

Fig 6.15 *The Lesser Antillean bullfinch occurs on most of the islands of the Eastern Caribbean but there are considerable inter-island differences in the plumage, especially in the males. This cock bird was photographed marauding the authors' breakfast in Antigua.*

Fig 6.16 *Black vultures scavenging dead fish on Maracas beach, Trinidad.*

7 Ecology and Conservation of Caribbean Seashores

A dictionary definition of the verb 'to conserve' includes to 'preserve; keep from harm, decay or loss'. This definition includes both a sense of maintaining the status quo and of protecting against degradation. Keeping habitats pristine is often not as simple as might be thought. Those left unaltered by man will reach stable states known as climax. These climax conditions will of course alter over the geological time scale but they are likely to be more or less stable for many millennia. Thus the islands of the Caribbean were mostly covered with one of a range of types of forest before Man arrived. In some of these islands only tiny remnants remain and in others even extensive forests may be very different in composition from those of a thousand years ago. In recent centuries there have been profound and continuous changes to the landscapes and seascapes of the region which have had widespread and mostly deleterious effects. In light of this a hope that habitats can be returned to their pristine, pre-human state is usually futile and some sort of compromise must be made. Thus conservation is often a case of preventing more detrimental changes and attempting perhaps to restore a little of the original condition. This is not usually just a matter of ring fencing areas against human influence. There is most often a need for active management

Fig 7.1 *Tourism is a huge source of revenue to the Caribbean region. However, from the conservation standpoint a high density of visitors can place stress on the natural environment.*

and creative inputs (as well as cash!). However, all conservation-minded individuals, we are sure, would agree that much can be done to rectify the damage and to activate plans that minimise future impacts. If possible any pristine or near pristine sites must be guarded and protected from damage.

Seashores are partially land and partially sea. The terrestrial habitat is relatively accessible and is thus often heavily affected by Man's presence. The marine element is somewhat less easily invaded by man and, although vulnerable, it usually avoids the worst abuses. However, the integrated nature of the ocean margin often means that a problem on land affects the sea and vice versa. Many conservationists recognise four strands to their work: namely, to address the issues of **pollution** and to protect **natural beauty, resources and wildlife**. Needless to say these factors often interact one with the other and there are frequently competing interests when trying to arrive at an optimal strategy.

Pollution

The Wider Caribbean Region (WCR) contains 24 island states and is bordered by 12 mainland countries having a population of 200 million with an estimated 100 million visitors each year. Most of the local population and virtually all of the tourist facilities are located near the sea. The islands alone receive about 12 million 'stay-over' tourists and about 8 million more from cruise ships. Having said that, the Caribbean region has relatively little industry and its agriculture is not so dependent on chemical inputs as that of many other parts of the world. Furthermore, the rivers that empty into the Caribbean Sea are fairly small and their influence can be more easily diluted than many other similar sized bodies of sea water (e.g. the Mediterranean Sea or the Gulf of Mexico). As a consequence the region suffers fewer environmental effects from anthropogenic (man-made) inputs than much of the rest of the world. None the less there are many worrying local problems and trends in addition to a number of global phenomena that threaten environmental quality. In respect of pollution and its control it is worth noting that materials entering the sea can do so in two main ways: from either a point source or a non-point source. The former is easy to identify (such as sewage pipe outfall) while the latter will include the drainage of groundwater into rivers and thence into the sea. Point sources are much easier to monitor and control, but sadly pollution from these is only a very small proportion of the whole.

Oil

The WCR produces about 170 million tonnes of oil per year – mainly in Columbia, Mexico, Trinidad and Tobago, the United States and Venezuela. Although the popular vision of oil pollution is one of vast wrecked tankers spilling their contents, the reality in the Caribbean is more mundane. Spills from tankers have occurred but they have been few in recent years and of relatively low impact. Rather the problems come from the intentional discharge of oil through bilge and tank washing, usually in breach of regulations. Gas and oil wells at sea also contribute to petrochemical contamination as do shore-based refineries and processing plants. This pollution, along with other factors, contributes to severe environmental effects in enclosed areas of sea which have poor circulation such as Kingston Harbour in Jamaica and Havana Bay, Cuba. Elsewhere more subtle effects are difficult to detect. Clearly oil deposition on coral can be fatal; seabirds that become coated are unlikely to survive and mangrove root fauna is susceptible to contact with particulate oil. However, we know little about the consequences of low levels of contamination.

Sewage

Some years ago the Pan American Health Organization (PAHO) estimated that in the Central American countries and the Caribbean islands only 10% of sewage was processed, the remainder being discharged untreated. More recently the PAHO surveyed 11 Caribbean states and found that sewage processing varied between 2% and 16%. Much of the untreated sewage is discharged directly into the sea, often down very short outfall pipes, while more sewage material will arrive in the sea via widely distributed seepage. The effects of these discharges are many and varied. Most obvious are the public health (disease transmission) concerns that arise either directly from the sea water or indirectly via contaminated marine food animals, in particular filter feeders such as bivalve molluscs. Other detrimental changes that can result include the degradation of coral reefs and seagrass beds. In severe cases this can be the result of direct contact between the sewage solids and the marine organisms. More usually the nutrient materials in the sewage encourage algal growth resulting in the swamping of the reef or seagrass bed biota. Of course the associated fisheries will suffer as a consequence. Sewage often contains a range of toxic materials including detergents from homes and businesses, tar-derived substances from road drains as well as heavy metals and a huge spectrum of chemicals from industry. Almost always regulations exist in respect of these discharges but just as frequently resources are not available for their policing and enforcement.

Building sophisticated sewage treatment plants is expensive and such capital projects may be too much of a financial challenge for some of the smaller countries. However, it has been achieved in some islands and much can be done with simpler systems including activated sludge package plants and even septic tanks. Sadly there is evidence to suggest that the processing plants that do exist are often under-maintained and inefficient, producing contaminated effluents.

Fig 7.2 *An underwater view of a typical seagrass bed.*

Silting

Marine animals and plants are often sensitive to suspended solids in the water which can affect them in a range of ways. Light penetration may be reduced and, if so, corals (which derive much energy from the photosynthesis of their symbiotic algae), seaweeds and seagrasses will suffer. Should the particulate material sediment out, then the silt can clog and suffocate delicate life forms especially filter and suspension feeders. Coral reef organisms, including the coral polyps, are extremely susceptible to such pollution and there are many examples of reefs either suffering loss of species or almost total destruction. Many of the suspended solids are the result of soil erosion which in turn has come about through deforestation or poor agriculture. Once hillsides are stripped of their trees the soil is vulnerable to being washed away by the rain into streams and rivers and eventually out to sea. Given that much Caribbean land is hilly or mountainous and that populations are often increasing, the tendency to exploit these steep slopes is not surprising. Although the consequences for the marine environment can be severe, they may be even worse for the agricultural resources; soil once lost is virtually impossible to replace. Unfortunately, sediments derived from agricultural soils will often have herbicides and pesticides bound to the particles further increasing the hazards to marine life. Another terrestrial source of suspended solids is the mining industry. Bauxite mining is to be found in a number of islands and is of great economic importance, for example, in Jamaica. Much is done at these mines to contain silt in settlement ponds and a bauxite loading quay shares Jamaica's Discovery Bay with the University of the West Indies Marine Laboratory (famous for its coral reef research) without apparent conflict.

Marine engineering works are also a source of suspended solids. The creation of marinas, dredged channels, sea walls and so on stirs up the seabed producing silt which will become deposited elsewhere resulting in the deleterious effects described above.

Agrochemicals

Mention has already been made of substances being bound to soil particles that have been washed out to sea but pesticide-, herbicide- and fertiliser-derived molecules will also arrive in the marine environment by direct runoff, either through streams and rivers or from groundwater seepage and sewage outfalls. The major concern in respect of the former two classes of compounds is that of bioaccumulation. Many of these chemicals are not metabolised but stored in the animals and plants. If they find their way into phytoplankton they will pass on their burden to the zooplankton that eats them. Predators that eat these zooplankton will, in turn, accumulate the chemical load of their prey and by the time they themselves are eaten by a top predator, such as a large fish or seabird, concentrations may have reached levels which are either toxic or can cause damaging effects. In such a system it is usually the top predators that will be most at risk. These will include large pelagic predatory fish, such as tuna or barracuda, fish-eating birds like the pelican and, of course, man. The brown pelican was particularly affected by pesticides in the 1960s. The large population on the Gulf coast of Louisiana declined to extinction largely due to the thinning of their eggshells as a direct result of ingested insecticides. The population on the Florida Gulf coasts did not decline in such a spectacular way, which was thought to be due to a lack of major rivers draining from that state. The Louisiana coast received very heavy amounts of pesticides because it is here that the Mississippi pours out water that has drained from much of the agricultural land of the central United States of America. Recognising the widespread problem posed by these chemicals, the US Environmental Protection Agency banned the use of DDT and dramatically reduced the use of endrin in 1972. Subsequently there have been reintroductions of pelicans and a sustained recovery in numbers. Luckily it appears that Caribbean pelicans have not been affected by pesticides; the US Fish and Wildlife Service website states: 'Pesticide residues, the primary cause of the decline of the eastern subspecies, were not high enough in the Caribbean to be considered hazardous'.[1] However, there is no cause for complacency and less obvious detrimental effects of pesticide pollution may lie undetected. The United Nations Environmental Programme's (UNEP) Assessment and Management of Environmental Pollution (AMEP) has a programme to help nations develop improved pesticide management (including runoff control). At the present time the emphasis is on the mainland countries of the Caribbean such as Nicaragua, Costa Rica, Panama and Columbia with their larger areas of agriculture and bigger rivers.

---

[1] http://endangered.fws.gov

Large predatory fishes seem to be relatively resistant to the direct effects of pollutants and the concern is more for the human consumers of such fish. Accumulation of toxins is not confined to pesticides and there has been a longstanding problem of heavy metal uptake by tuna. Mercury in particular is retained within the fish's tissues and this can then be passed on to those who eat them. However, as with pesticides, the Caribbean does not seem to be a region where high mercury levels are found in fish. A greater danger to those who eat fish comes from cigatura poisoning. The toxin originates in a microscopic alga that occurs on reefs. It passes through the food chain, being accumulated in top predators in just the same way as pesticides. The fish themselves are immune to the toxin but humans eating the fish can be affected with a range of symptoms from sickness and diarrhoea to long-lasting neurological problems and, in very severe cases, death. The disease occurs throughout the tropics where reef fish are eaten. In the Caribbean it is most often reported on the larger islands but the statistics are likely to be untrustworthy due to many cases going undiagnosed. The minuscule dinoflagellate that produces the toxin lives attached to larger seaweeds and there is some evidence that anything that favours more growth of these on the reef will increase the risk of poisoning occurring. The widespread death of corals around the world, which has resulted in greater seaweed cover of reefs, may suggest that cigatura poisoning is likely to increase in the future.

The entry of agricultural fertilisers, especially nitrates and phosphates, into the sea via runoff tends to promote marine plant growth. If the increased growth is excessive eutrophication can occur. When this happens algal growth is stimulated by the added nutrients leading to overgrowth of the normal sedentary animals and plants accompanied by a fall in dissolved oxygen. Obviously this process can degrade reefs and seagrass beds. In enclosed areas of sheltered harbours and bays this can be very severe while on open coasts the effects may be less dramatic but nevertheless important in altering inshore ecosystems.

Solid waste

We live in an age of packaging and, even worse, of non-biodegradable packaging. Substantial amounts of this material and other mainly plastic items find their way into the sea only to reappear, washed up on the beach. Many tourist beaches are so inundated with these unsightly materials that they have to be 'cleaned' each day (usually clearing away interesting shells at the same time). On less frequented beaches the material simply accumulates. Education and community programmes are nibbling away at the problem but the challenge is huge. Some of the garbage is a hazard to wildlife either through animals ingesting it or by their becoming entangled in it. Sadly there is evidence to suggest that much of the solid waste in the sea comes from ships, either from fishing boats discarding tangled line and broken nets and floats or from cruise ships which generate large amounts of rubbish.

Ideally this should be discharged at the ports visited but frequently these do not even have sufficient facility to dispose of their own local waste let alone cope with the additional load from the liners. To store the total amount of waste from the whole trip for eventual disposal in the home port is often regarded as unrealistic and so, despite some successful prosecutions, dumping at sea does take place.

Fig 7.3 *Plastics and many other man-made materials are both buoyant and persistent. They may accumulate on beaches to unacceptable levels. Not only are these objects an eyesore but they also constitute a hazard to wildlife on the beach and in the sea.*

Natural beauty

The conservation of natural beauty is primarily aimed at preserving landscapes and seascapes with a particular aesthetic appeal. In the context of this book, greatest concern revolves around the issues of seaside development. There is here, as in many other related problems, a complex conflict of interests. Coastal scenery of great beauty attracts tourists; the local government and commercial interests wish to cater for those tourists through the provision of a wide range of facilities from hotels and restaurants to banks and boating. Ironically the provision of even the simplest of these services starts to compromise the natural beauty and this process increases as the provision extends. Only through great self-control and discipline on the part of the planners and builders can the delicate tightrope be walked. What makes the decisions more difficult is that there is no common agreement or absolute measure of beauty. Furthermore, there is a great desire to have one's cake and eat it; the local resident wishes to derive an income from tourism but not have his homeland altered for the worse; the tourist desires to visit beautiful places but wishes that the hotels and amenities existed for him alone, unspoiled by hordes of like-minded travellers. A large proportion of this book's readers will themselves be fuelling the building of yet more hotels and marinas by their presence in these lovely places and through their requirement for high standards of accommodation. There is also the question of other non-tourist and industrial developments which frequently take place near the sea. Clearly these are matters which can be most successfully dealt with by clear minded and strictly enforced planning regulations and permissions. We think most visitors from Europe and the United States would agree that Caribbean resorts have escaped the worst excesses seen in some parts of the Mediterranean or Florida, but that is not to say that there are no eyesores or examples of seaside gems ruined by greed and ambition.

The principles of good planning are of course a long way outside our expertise and it would be impertinent for us to preach to the professionals. However, it does seem to us that there are some simple features that 'good' (whatever that means) planning have in common. Firstly, it makes sense to set aside outstanding examples of landscape to be free of all development (other than that for day visitors, information centres, car parks and so on). Secondly (and here the Caribbean has been largely successful), seaside buildings should be low and set back as far as possible from the beach itself. Thirdly, if there must be large tourist developments then let them be as compact as possible and as well hidden from other parts of the coastline as can be designed. In this regard coastlines with deeply indented bays (such as Antigua) fare better than those that are more or less straight (like Barbados). Finally, if buildings have to be built then let them complement rather than clash with their surroundings and let much thought (and funds) be given to the landscaping and planting of the grounds.

Fig 7.4 *There are many sites in the Caribbean which could be developed for tourism but the changes that would be wrought could well destroy the initial attraction.*

Resources

As has been mentioned in the previous section conflicts will always arise whenever a space is used or exploited by different groups of people for different reasons. Underlying any acceptable plan for the use of Caribbean beaches and shores must be a resolution of those differences. Leonard Nurse, presently Permanent Secretary Environment in Barbados, said in an interview about the implementation of coastal management on that island, 'We have a number of competing user groups – the tourism sector; hoteliers; fisheries; and water-sport operators such as jet-ski and glass-bottom boat operators. Conflict resolution became a new and emerging issue.'[2] We would add to that list those representing the environmental and conservation priorities.

At many sites throughout the Caribbean overfishing of inshore stocks has produced deleterious and far-reaching effects on shallow water habitats. Fishing these waters can be a low-tech operation using simple wood and chicken-wire traps or snorkel and speargun. Where such operations are intensive the effects are easily seen in that fish longer than a few centimetres are absent and the numbers are reduced. This lower total biomass of fish has a number of knock-on effects. Perhaps most important is the reduction of grazing by herbivorous fish which normally constitute a large proportion of

[2] Intercoast Network, Winter 1999, p12

Fig 7.5 *One of the biggest difficulties in trying to draft environmental policy for Caribbean beaches is resolving the differences that arise between the various interests. Thus boat and diving operations may conflict with fishermen and those anxious to conserve coral reefs. Inter-group discussion and sensible codes of practice can do much to defuse potentially contentious situations.*

Fig 7.6 *The importance of fisheries to the local communities must not be overlooked and sustainability should be encouraged. This picture shows final stages of a seine net haul in Tobago; this operation requires a considerable amount of cooperation between the individual fishermen.*

the population. Relatively unchecked, seaweeds and other algae spread over the reefs and hard substrates displacing corals. Although other factors have produced a similar end result in recent years (see below), there is no doubt that reefs depleted of their fish have suffered especially badly. As reefs are the key to high biodiversity and high biological production, these changes are undoubtedly bad by any measure. Apart from the biological effects, degraded reefs produce less fish for the local human population than a reef cropped in a sustainable way and are much less attractive to diving and snorkelling tourists. Reefs lacking live coral are subject to more rapid erosion than live reefs, rendering the enclosed lagoons or protected beaches much more vulnerable to wave and storm damage.

Many West Indian nations have marine parks or protected areas but in the face of widespread unemployment and low incomes policing these is difficult as is the enforcement of fishing regulations. Much is being attempted through social and economic programmes to educate local fisherpeople towards less intensive fishing using the concept of higher sustainable catches as the potential reward. For example there have been mesh exchange schemes in Jamaica whereby enough 3.8 cm ($1\frac{1}{2}$ in) wire mesh for two traps was handed out in exchange for each trap with 2.5 cm (1 in) mesh. Of course these initiatives require funding not only for the materials but also for the education elements which are essential for long-term success. In islands with a small population or a fairly high per capita income, the establishment of

Fig 7.7 *An underwater view of seaweed growing on a coral reef. Weed growth on reefs has increased in recent decades (see text).*

marine parks has produced beneficial effects on reefs and the associated ecosystems. One of the best known examples is that of Bonaire in the Dutch Antilles. Since 1979 the waters around the island from high water mark to a depth of 60 m (200 ft) have been designated a marine park protected by law. Fishing by the local population is at a low level and it is thought that the major impacts result from tourism that mainly caters for diving and watersports. Direct effects on submarine habitats are fairly low but the indirect effects from added nutrients (derived from sewage treatment) and silting are probably of greater importance. The fact that 25 000 divers were attracted to Bonaire in 1994 is testament to the excellent condition of the reefs.

Fig 7.8 *Fish traps like this one are efficient but unselective. When overused (especially with small mesh netting) they can rapidly reduce reef-fish populations with many knock-on effects.*

Wildlife

'Within the wider Caribbean region, there is consensus that coastal marine systems are changing for the worse.'[3] This statement was made in the Introduction to the first full report of the Caribbean Coastal Marine Productivity Program (CARICOMP), an organisation involving some 27 marine institutions in 17 countries dedicated to a standardised survey of the region's inshore marine ecosystems. As the report discusses, it is extremely difficult to disentangle the effects due to Man's activities and the ravages of Nature. None the less there can be no doubt that there is huge pressure from local coastal-zone populations (estimated at 100 million people and thought to be likely to double in the next 30 years). Add to this a rapidly increasing tourist industry and the size of the actual and potential environmental threat becomes obvious.

[3] Kjerfve *et al.*, *Caribbean coral reefs, seagrass and mangrove sites*, UNESCO, 1998, p. 2

Fig 7.9 *The desire to take home shells as souvenirs is very great. Collecting the shells of already dead animals does no harm but sadly shell stalls like this one will be displaying shells collected while their occupants were still alive. Over-collection will eventually lead to population decline of these beautiful molluscs. Remember, too, that trade in some items is illegal and attempts to import them into the United States and Great Britain could land the carrier in trouble.*

The single biggest threat to seashore wildlife comes from habitat destruction. The three major inshore ecosystems of coral reefs, mangrove swamps and seagrass beds are all under attack either deliberately or caught in a crossfire between exploitation and competing pressures. Let us briefly consider each.

Coral reefs

During the past two or three decades reefs worldwide have been subjected to a range of problems. In 1987 there was widespread bleaching of coral in the Caribbean when coral polyps shed their symbiotic algae – an act that led in many cases to death of the coral tissue. This stress-induced reaction was thought to have been triggered by high summer seawater temperatures, perhaps a manifestation of global warming. Other similar bleaching events have occurred in the Caribbean and elsewhere since that time and repetition in the future is likely. Whatever the primary cause, increased sediments in the waters over the reefs (see above) seem to have operated synergistically to maximise damage. A range of other problems have also damaged coral reefs since the 1970s. Various diseases have infected the corals themselves. In particular white-band disease has attacked species of *Acropora* and black-band disease has infected the massive *Montastrea* and *Diploria* species.

Once again environmental stresses may have exacerbated the microbial infections. Another disease led to the death of over 90% of the long-spined black sea urchin, *Diadema antillarum*, in the 1980s. This urchin grazes algae on reefs and its removal resulted in seaweeds competing more actively for space with settling coral juveniles as well as causing damage to established corals through abrasion. As mentioned above, overfishing of herbivorous fish and increased nutrient levels resulting from discharge and runoff have had similar effects. Anyone who knew the reefs of the Caribbean 30 years ago would be instantly aware of their present depleted nature although there are small signs here and there of fresh coral settlement and regeneration.

In some cases nearshore reefs have been demolished to make boat channels or in the mistaken belief that the quality of the beach would be improved. The effects are usually quite the reverse and the removal of the reef's protective role leads to large waves breaking on the beach which erode its sand. The same thing happens if reefs are badly damaged by hurricanes or tropical storms. Examples of beach destruction can be seen throughout the Caribbean and one can see that subsequent storms will be much more likely to threaten not only what remains of the beach but also the beach-side buildings and their inhabitants.

For the beachcomber the reduction in quality or disappearance of offshore reefs will affect both the richness of the finds at the tideline and probably render the beach itself steeper, narrower and composed of coarser sand.

Fig 7.10 *A considerable amount of sand has been removed from this west coast Barbados beach as evidenced by the exposed roots of the manchineel trees.*

Mangrove swamps

Much has already been said in this and earlier chapters about the role of mangrove swamps as buffer zones between land and sea, as nursery grounds for a wide range of deeper water species and as an exploitable resource for food, wood and other items. Despite a widespread understanding of these benefits to both Man and the environment generally, mangrove swamps continue to be destroyed in the name of 'progress'. They are often regarded as ugly or simply as 'a waste of space' that could be better used for some form of development. Certainly it is more difficult to persuade would-be developers of the case to conserve mangroves than, say, sandy beaches or coral reefs. None the less the fight must, and does, go on. Education and the establishment of more protected areas are increasing the chances for survival of the remaining swamps. There are even attempts being made in various places to re-establish stands of red mangrove.

Fig 7.11 *Mangrove swamps can be exploited in a sustainable way by small groups of fishermen although larger operations would be likely to threaten not only swamp fish populations but also recruitment to the reefs.*

Fig 7.12 *In some places attempts are being made to restore or establish mangroves. Here, in Tortola, BVI, young red mangrove trees have been planted in plastic tubes for protection.*

Seagrass beds

Like mangrove swamps, seagrass beds act as a buffer between land and sea, protecting each from the other. They also have a similar role as a protected environment in which juvenile sea life can grow. Compared with the other two major habitats, seagrass beds have fared relatively well in the face of Man's invasion of the region. Of course they have not been immune to the effects of pollution, dredging and the removal of or damage to offshore reefs. Changes in sand deposition can result in seagrasses being covered and recovery is slow at best.

Overall there is concern for these crucial marine habitats. Most importantly the nearshore marine system works best when these three major elements work in a fully integrated way. To quote again from the CARICOMP report, 'some of the most productive areas along tropical and subtropical coasts are found where broad seagrass meadows are interposed between the mangrove and coral reef communities'. Progress is being made in raising environmental issues up the priority ladder when resource conflicts arise and there is a greater understanding that well managed marine habitats will be advantageous to the great majority of the interested parties. However, much needs to be done in gathering reliable data upon which to base recommendations. Perhaps most importantly policy makers as well as those who live in or visit the Caribbean need to be made fully aware of the requirement to protect and, if possible, improve the quality of the natural world around them.

Fig 7.13 *This aerial view of Coral Cove, Grenada, shows a coral reef with a seagrass bed inshore of it. In earlier times, mangroves may well have grown behind the beach; they still do grow in less exposed bays out of sight to the upper right. Integration between these three major inshore communities results in the richest flora and fauna combined with high productivity.*

8 Looking at Seashores

Safety

By and large Caribbean beaches are fairly free of hazard; tides are small, the climate and sea temperatures are benign, visibility is usually good and storms are infrequent (but see page 8). None the less it pays to be aware of potential dangers and take appropriate action. Although residents and frequent visitors might be more aware of the problems, there is always the danger of familiarity breeding contempt.

- **Clothing** is important especially when on rocks or in swamps. It is very unwise to walk in either without sensible shoes. Bare feet offer little protection against rocks or shell fragments that can be razor sharp. In swamps broken roots and branches as well as cans and bottles can be obscured by the often opaque water. Flip-flop (thong) sandals tend to grip the surface but permit the foot to slide within them – a recipe for disaster on rock. We find that a pair of old trainers give good grip combined with support and protection. The same applies when paddling even in shallow water where coral and rocks are mixed with sand. A hat and perhaps a T-shirt are sensible additions to swimwear unless you are fully accustomed to the tropical sun; beachcombing is an addictive practice and hours can go by before you realise that your dreamt-of tan is going to disappear in shreds of scarlet skin. Don't forget the sunscreen. If you plan to be searching for long, then carrying a bottle of water is a good idea.

- **Waves** on exposed shores can be dangerous. You can be lulled into a sense of false security only to be knocked over by the 'big one'. On rock platforms that can mean being washed over sharp rocks often housing urchins by the hundred. We have spent considerable amounts of time treating the gashes and embedded spines resulting from such accidents, which are far from rare. Worse still, one could be pulled back into the sea with disastrous results. If you wish to collect or observe in such places it is wise to have a wave-watching companion to shout out warnings. Incidentally, cuts and grazes that you pick up in the field should be treated carefully with antiseptic and dressings as in the tropical climate infections can quickly develop. It is certainly wise to have a small first-aid kit to hand.

- **Shore and shallow-water animals** and a few **seashore plants** are hazardous. A number of sponges, especially red ones, can deliver nasty stings. Jellyfish and jellyfish-like animals have stinging tentacles. The one

Fig 8.1 *Many rocky shores in the Caribbean are on limestone which is easily eroded to produce a surface full of sharp points and with many small holes; a hazardous surface on which to walk. Note also how this shore has been undercut by the waves which, because of the small tides, tend to break always at the same height.*

most likely to be met is the Portuguese man-of-war. Fire corals are common on shallow reefs together with the long-spined black sea urchin. A number of seaside plants are toxic to various extents. The seeds of some plants in the pea family are poisonous (especially red and black ones) and the 'apples' of the manchineel contain a very corrosive toxin, which also washes off the leaves during rain – not a tree to shelter under. More detail of these animals and plants can be found elsewhere in this book.

Fig 8.2 *Manchineel trees often grow on or near seashores. This notice spells out the hazards.*

- **Alcohol** does not help you to act sensibly on, in or near the sea. Indeed there are many examples, some tragic, of alcohol clouding people's judgement. Rum, beer and other drinks are readily and cheaply available in the West Indies and, given the climate, the temptation to over-indulge is always there. If it is a temptation you can't resist then at least wait until you are safely(?) seated on a bar stool.
- **Personal security** is not usually a problem in the Caribbean but be aware of local conditions. If you are new to an area ask about where you should or should not go and (if this applies) about the advisability of going alone. If you plan to be out for a long time or in a remote area let someone know of your plans before you leave. Visitors from the United Kingdom and continental Europe should know that their mobile phones are unlikely to function in the region, as the system used is that of the US cellphone.

Observing

The most obvious way to beachcomb is simply to walk along the **strandline** of a sandy beach and see what you find. The strandline may in fact be more than one line. Material will accumulate at the point where the waves are presently reaching while further up the beach other lines will mark various high tides and often, way back in the undergrowth, there will be items deposited during storms. Some beaches will immediately yield interesting things; others will be virtually sterile. It is difficult to predict how productive any given beach will be but those with seagrass beds or coral reefs offshore are usually worth a visit. For any given beach the best pickings will be after

Fig 8.3 *Four specimens of Nutting's vase shell. This gastropod is rare in the Caribbean except in parts of Antigua where these specimens were found. All were collected on the strandline but only one is recently dead. The other three show very considerable wear although enough of their original form remains to allow an identification.*

storms when all sorts of interesting animals and plants will have been dislodged. In resort areas a sense of excessive tidiness sometimes prevails and tractors 'sweep' the beach each day collecting up all the 'rubbish'. This makes strandline collecting somewhat frustrating but if you can find where they deposit the so-called 'rubbish' much walking on the beach will be saved. Strandline specimens may have been in the water for a considerable period of time before being washed up. They can be anything between mildly abraded to worn so smooth as to be unrecognisable. Furthermore, you may only retrieve part of the specimen, perhaps just a claw or part of a valve. If your interest is purely aesthetic this might be no problem, indeed the object may be enhanced by its treatment. But those who wish to identify isolated parts to a species will find themselves becoming detectives. There is great satisfaction in, for example, being able to identify a semicircle of shell as the posterior segment of a chiton. ('Or is it a gastropod operculum? … or perhaps a broken piece of scallop shell?' The debate goes on and for this, if not for field collecting, alcohol seems to assist the process.)

Fig 8.4 *Shells washed up on a beach like this are likely to have been harshly treated as not only will the sand abrade them but, in the heavy surf, the stones and coral debris will inflict more severe damage.*

Fig 8.5 *These bits and pieces which cover a wide diversity of animal and plant groups were collected on a Jamaican beach in just a few minutes. Many collectors will be happy to enjoy their aesthetic qualities but others will take great pleasure from attempting to identify them.*

On **bedrock beaches** the organisms will mostly be alive and Chapter 3 on rocky shores should help you understand what they are and how they live. What if you see a live snail with a nice shell – should you add it to your collection? If it is a common animal then dead shells should be available nearby; if it is uncommon then it certainly should not be removed. Either way the advice must be 'no' except for the most serious of scientific reasons. Remember too that collecting and/or removal from the country may be illegal (depends on local laws) and importation of certain biological materials into your home country may also breach national or international regulations. Such restrictions do not usually apply to 'already dead when found' items but you may need to check locally. **Boulder beaches** offer the opportunity of turning over rocks to see what lies underneath. The differences between the upper and lower surfaces of rocks are striking but hardly surprising. The tops are exposed to wave action as well as to the drying and heating effects of the tropical sun. Beneath is cool, damp and protected from many sorts of predator. Lifting such rocks reveals this hidden world. It is of vital importance that you replace the rock as near as possible to its original position. Almost the worst sin a beachcomber can commit is to leave stones and rocks the wrong way up because most of the inhabitants of both surfaces will perish. Soft and delicate structures from below will be seared in the sun while those now underneath will be denied access to light and air (and open water when the tide and waves wash over them).

Fig 8.6 *This shows the undersurface of a rock on the beach shown in Fig 3.4 (page 56). The community of delicate life-forms includes attached animals such as sponges, anemones, annelid worms, bivalves and tunicates as well as more mobile gastropods and sea urchins. If this rock is not returned to its original position most of these creatures will quickly perish.*

Visiting **mangrove swamps** varies from difficult to relatively easy. The easiest and most instructive way is probably to take a guided boat trip such as exist for visitors to the Caroni Swamp (Trinidad) and the Black River (Jamaica). The boat operators are not only knowledgeable about the swamp and its flora and fauna, but also travelling by boat is much the best way in such places. Smaller swamps such as exist in many of the islands can sometimes be approached from the shore side but unless there are paths they are often difficult to penetrate (see Fig 4.5 on page 92). If it is possible to arrange one, a local guide can make the mangrove expedition more rewarding. Footwear is, once more, an important item and insect repellent is usually essential. Despite the problems of getting into and around swamps they undoubtedly offer a rich and novel experience, especially for 'first timers'.

It is well worth while to consider a **night trip** to the shore. Many animals that hide away or are inactive during the day are more active at night (for example many of the limpets will be on the move). Others (e.g. Sally Lightfoot crabs) are more easily approached using torchlight than by day. The ultimate night time beach watch must be to see female turtles hauling themselves out for egg laying. Many hotels with turtle beaches nearby organise trips on nights when turtles are active. Clearly for such forays a torch is essential and extra care needs to be taken on rocky shores after dark.

Fig 8.7 *Boat trips into mangrove swamps are usually easily arranged in the larger swamps. This group in Trinidad's Caroni Swamp are waiting for the evening flight of scarlet ibis.*

Collecting and identification

Many beachcombers will want to collect and keep a sample of the better specimens that they find. Providing that one takes only dead specimens (bearing in mind the points raised above about local and international restrictions) this is a perfectly natural and reasonable impulse. Better still there will probably also be a desire to identify what has been collected. Such active engagement with the natural world can only strengthen an understanding of the need to protect and conserve the seashore habitats which are threatened in so many ways.

For **collecting** one needs little by way of equipment. A small plastic tea strainer is sometimes useful for sifting through mud and fine sand and a small trowel can be employed on the same substrates. Some advise taking hammers and even small crowbars on to rocky beaches, both to remove attached animals and to open up cracks and crevices. In our view such

Fig 8.8 *Beachcombing may be dull and frustrating sometimes but finds like this thorny oyster can make it all worth while.*

destructive collection can only be justified for serious scientific investigations. A hand lens is worth having but it really comes into its own later during the identification stage. Try to get into the habit of taking field notes about what was found where and when. It also pays to put items, or groups of items, in plastic bags with labels (pencil writing survives dampness better than most pens). For transport the bags can be carried in sandwich boxes which will protect delicate specimens.

Identifying the material you have collected is sometimes easy, sometimes difficult, and, occasionally, especially with beach-worn items, almost impossible. In the previous pages we have tried to introduce you to the most likely candidates but of course this is only the tip of the iceberg. Those who get hooked on naming *all* of their collection may need to consult the list of mostly more specialised books in the Bibliography. Many local museums have named reference collections of shells for comparison with your specimens; however it is wise to be cautious, as it is not unknown for one or two items in these collections to be mislabelled! A hand lens is useful when working on the smaller shells, flowers and seaweeds. For most things, **preservation** is a simple matter. All that shells need is a careful wash but make sure they are thoroughly dry before storing. Most flowers and leaves can be pressed between sheets of newspaper and many fruits and seeds can be dried and stored in plastic bags. Soft seaweeds can often be spread on plain paper and dried in the sun; their own slippery secretions will act as glue to hold them in place. Calcareous seaweeds can be dried but must be stored with care as they are often fragile. If you feel you are justified in collecting live molluscs for their shells then the best strategy is to kill them by placing them in cold water and heating it to boiling point (said to be more humane than plunging into hot water). Drain and cool, then remove the soft part as completely as possible (a needle works quite well for small snails, a tooth pick for larger ones).

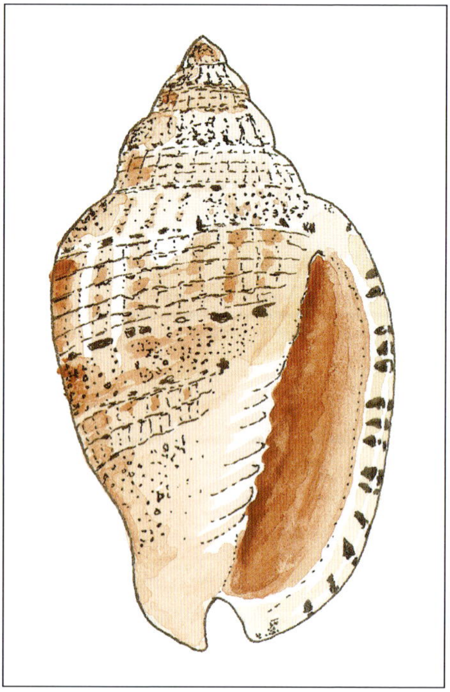

Fig 8.9 *Take a waterproof drawing pen and paints with you on the collecting trips. The music volute may not be as accurately reproduced as in a photograph but this illustration did require a concentrated examination of the specimen.*

However, be warned; it is difficult to remove all the flesh from snails and putrefaction is rapid in the tropics. You will probably not want to preserve soft-bodied animals (or shells complete with flesh), but if the need arises alcohol is as good as anything. If it is undiluted (as in methylated spirits) then add about 1 volume of water to 2 parts of spirit before using. In extreme situations rum works well, at least temporarily; after all, that's what they brought Nelson home in after the Battle of Trafalgar (some say it was brandy but the principle is the same).

Drawing and painting specimens is also a good way of recording what you find and the results take less space than a shell collection. It is well worth while keeping a paint box to hand; a waterproof drawing pen is also useful as it produces a better outline than a pencil. The act of drawing objects makes you look at them with great attention giving you a better understanding of how they are put together as well as sharpening your observational skills. You may doubt your artistic ability, but give it a try and you will probably be surprised how satisfying the results can be.

Exploring the submarine world

This book is designed for those who are interested in the natural history of beaches and the animal and plant remains that are washed up on seashores. For many this may be enough. For others there will be a desire to know more about the living world below the waves. There are various ways in which one can explore these submarine wonders and if you have not already ventured forth here are a few suggestions. Many resorts have **glass-bottomed boats**. These permit passengers to examine the seabed from the comfort of a seat without getting wet at all. Mostly these trips are over shallow coral reefs (such as at Buccoo Reef, Tobago) and the views can be spectacular. The quality of the commentary from the local operators (in respect of the biology) is variable (but usually excellent) and the trips are worth while for those who do not snorkel or dive. The same effect as that given by these boats can be achieved on a miniature scale with a box or bucket in which glass or clear plastic has replaced the bottom. Such viewing boxes when held in the water abolish the disturbed sea surface that makes looking at the seabed difficult even in the calmest conditions.

The next step is to **snorkel**. This technique employs a glass-fronted mask over the eyes and nose and a snorkel (breathing tube) held in the mouth. With these it is easy to float over the seabed, face down, breathing as you go. Fins help with the swimming but are very much optional unless you graduate to diving down to get a closer look. Some hotels and dive shops run snorkelling courses but most people find it an easy skill to master by themselves. If you don't already possess a mask buy one from a reputable dive gear store; face shapes vary and you may need some help to find one that fits well as there is nothing more annoying than a mask that leaks. This is even more true if you take up **SCUBA diving**. If you wish to learn to dive then the Caribbean is the place to start. Everything is so much easier in warm water, with good visibility and unencumbered with the sort of suit you would need in a temperate climate. There are usually plenty of well qualified operators taking beginners on to internationally recognised Professional Association of Diving Instructors (PADI) courses and some islands have British Sub Aqua Club (BSAC) branches which also teach diving to the standard of their qualifications. The latter will take longer than PADI and are more suited to residents or long-term visitors. However, be warned, diving is heavily addictive, especially in Caribbean conditions! That said, there is no better or more enjoyable way to experience and strive to understand the complexities of shallow water environments.

Fig 8.10 *Beachcombing can be fascinating and challenging, but for many people a close-up view of marine life is their goal. If so, then SCUBA diving is the answer.*

Bibliography

The following is not a list of sources but a selection of more specialised texts mostly concerned with the identification of seashore plants and animals.

Abbott, R.T. and Morris, P.A. (1994) *Field Guide to the Shells of the Atlantic* (Peterson Field Guide). Houghton Mifflin. ISBN 0-395-69779-4. (Includes coverage of Gulf coasts and the West Indies.)

Carrington, S. (1998) *Wild Plants of the Eastern Caribbean.* Macmillan Education. ISBN 0-333-67443-X.

Evans, P. (1990) *Birds of the Eastern Caribbean.* Macmillan Education. ISBN 0-333-52155-2.

Jones, A. and Sefton, N. (2002) *Marine Life of the Caribbean.* Macmillan Education. ISBN 0-333-93048-7. (Takes the reader from the seashore into deeper water.)

Kaplan, E.H. (1988) *Southeastern and Caribbean Sea Shores* (Peterson Field Guide). Houghton Mifflin. ISBN 0-395-97516-6. (A very inclusive but rather crowded book with emphasis on US coasts.)

Littler, D.C., Littler, M.M., Bucher, K.E. and Norris, J.N. (1989) *Marine Plants of the Caribbean.* Smithsonian Institution. ISBN 0-874-74607-8. (Covers seaweeds and seagrasses.)

Nellis, D.W. (1994) *Seashore Plants of Southern Florida and the Caribbean.* Pineapple Press. ISBN 0-156-164056-5.

Raffaele, H. et al (1998) *Birds of the West Indies.* Christopher Helm. ISBN 0-713-64905-4. (Comprehensive but relatively expensive guide to identifying the region's avifauna.)

Sutty, L. (1990) *Seashells of the Caribbean.* Macmillan Education. ISBN 0-333-52191-9.

Voss, G.L. (2002) *Seashore Life of Florida and the Caribbean.* Dover Publications. ISBN 0-486-42068-X (A reprint of the book that originally appeared in 1976. Generally good but omits any coverage of shelled molluscs.)

Two other books to consider are:

Redfern, C. (2001) *Bahamian Sea Shells.* Available from www.Bahamianseashells.com (ISBN 0-971-10660-6). (A beautifully produced book but presently only obtainable via the website and expensive at US$114 plus delivery.)

Warmke, G.L. and Abbott, R.T. (1961). *Caribbean Seashells.* Livingston. (An excellent book sadly out of print but copies fairly common on the second-hand market.)

Common and Scientific Names

Introduction

Throughout this book we have used common names where there is one in currency. However, it has to be recognised that in some cases there may be problems with this. In English there is often more than one such name (although usually simple variations on a theme). Multiplicity of names is complicated by the fact that many other languages and dialects than English exist in the Caribbean and some creatures will have common names in all of them. Thus the use of scientific names is the safest way of knowing which animal or plant is being referred to. These names are in two parts (binomial nomenclature): the first name is that of the genus and the second is that of the species within that genus. For example the bivalve Florida jewel box has the scientific name of *Charma florida*. The foliate jewel box is so closely related that it is in the same genus but, of course, is a different species and its name is *Charma macerophylla*. If there is uncertainty about the species only the genus name, often followed by 'sp.', is used, as for example, the fiddler crab, *Uca* sp. Conventionally these names are written in italics with the first letter of the generic name in capital and the first letter of the specific name in lower case.

When new species are described in the scientific literature they are given their binomial and this then becomes their ONLY name in science. The snag about these names (apart from having to remember them) is that scientists frequently revise them in light of new research. In the text (page 71) we have referred to such a case with the winkles and periwinkles where we now know that one 'old' species is in fact many 'new' species and not only that but they have been assigned to a new genus too. These changes take some time to feed through into popular science publications so you will still find some variations between scientific names in older and newer books. None the less the scientific name is still the one least likely to cause confusion.

Crustaceans

barnacle, goose	*Lepus antifera*
barnacle, ribbed	*Tetraclita stalactifera*
barnacle, star	*Chthamalus* sp.
crab, blue	*Callinectes sapidus*
crab, calico	*Eriphia gonagra*
crab, common box	*Calappa gallus*

crab, fiddler	*Uca* sp.
crab, flame box	*Calappa flammea*
crab, ghost	*Ocypode quadrata*
crab, hermit	*Pagurus* sp. and others
crab, mangrove	*Goniopsis cruentata*
crab, mud	*Panopeus herbstii*
crab, Sally Lightfoot	*Grapsus grapsus*
crab, granulated spider	*Mithrax verrucosus*
crab, spiny actaea	*Actaea acantha*
crab, tree	*Aratus pisonii*
lobster, spiny	*Panulirus argus*
mantis shrimp	*Squilla empusa*

Molluscs (bivalves)

aphis, gaudy	*Asaphis deflorata*
ark, eared	*Anadara notabilis*
ark, white reticulated	*Barbatia domingensis*
cockle, Atlantic strawberry	*Americardia media*
cockle, yellow	*Trachycardium muricatum*
donax, Caribbean	*Donax denticulatus*
jewel box, Florida	*Charma florida*
jewel box, foliate	*C. macerophylla*
lima	*Lima scabra*
lucine, Pennsylvania	*Lucina pensylvanica*
lucine, thick	*Phacoides pectinatus*
microcockle, pink	*Microcardium tinctum*
mussel, green	*Perna viridis*
mussel, scorched	*Hormomya exusta*
mussel, yellow	*Ischadium citrinus*
oyster, Atlantic pearl	*Pinctada radiata*
oyster, Atlantic thorny	*Spondylus americanus*
oyster, Atlantic wing	*Pteria colymbus*
oyster, 'coon	*Lopha frons*
oyster, flat tree	*Isognomon alatus*
oyster, Lister's tree	*I. radiatus*
oyster, mangrove	*Crassostrea rhizophorae*
pen shell, amber	*Pinna carnea*
tellin, pink thin	*Tellina exilis*
tivela, trigonal	*Tivella mactroides*
turkey wing	*Arca zebra*
venus, beaded	*Chione granulata*
venus, cross barred	*C. cancellata*

venus, king	*C. paphia*
venus, princess	*Antigona listeri*
venus, rigid	*A. rigida*
venus, West Indian pointed	*Anomalocardia brasiliana*

Molluscs (gastropods and other non-bivalves)

bubble shell, striated	*Bulla striata*
cantharus, common	*Cantharus auritulus*
cerith, awl miniature	*Cerithiopsis emersoni*
cerith, ivory	*Cerithium eburneum*
cerith, middlespined	*C. algicola*
cerith, stocky	*C. litteratum*
chiton, fuzzy	*Acanthopleura granulata*
chiton, West Indian	*Chiton tuberculatus*
conch, queen	*Strombus gigas*
conch, rooster tail	*S. gallus*
conch, West Indian fighting	*S. pugilis*
cone, glory of the Atlantic	*Conus granulatus*
cone, mouse	*C. mus*
cone, West Indian alphabet	*C. spurius*
cowrie helmet shell	*Cypraecassis testiculus*
cowrie, Atlantic grey	*Cypraea cinerea*
cowrie, Atlantic yellow	*C. spurca acicularis*
cowrie, coffee bean	*Trivia pediculus*
cowrie, measled	*Cypraea zebra*
dove shell, common	*Columbella mercatoria*
dove shell, smooth	*Nitidella laevigata*
false limpet, Goe's	*Trimusculus goesi*
flamingo tongue	*Cyphoma gibbosum*
frog-shell	*Bursa* sp.
hoof shell	*Hipponix* sp.
latirus, chestnut	*Leucozonia nassa*
limpet, Barbados keyhole	*Fissurella barbadensis*
limpet, eight-ribbed	*Hemitoma octoradiata*
limpet, green keyhole	*Diodora viridula*
limpet, knobby keyhole	*Fissurella nodosa*
moon shell, brown	*Polinices hepaticus*
murex, apple	*Chicoreus brevifrons*
murex, West Indian	*C. pomum*
music volute	*Voluta musica*
natica	*Natica* sp.
nerite, bloody-toothed	*Nerita peloronta*

nerite, four-toothed	*N. versicolor*
nerite, tessellated	*N. tesselata*
olive, netted	*Oliva reticularis*
periwinkle, beaded	*Tectarius muricatus*
periwinkle, dwarf	*Nodilittorina mespillum*
periwinkle, mangrove	*Littoraria angulifera*
periwinkle, spotted	*Nodilittorina melagris*
planaxis,black Atlantic	*Planaxis nucleus*
planaxis, striped	*P. lineatus*
prickly-winkle, common	*Nodilittorina tuberculata*
prickly-winkle, false	*Tectarius antonii*
purpura, wide-mouthed	*Purpura patula*
rock shell, Florida	*Thais haemastoma floridana*
sea hare, ragged	*Bursatella leachi plei*
sea hare, spotted	*Aplysia dactylomela*
sea slug, rough	*Pleurobranchus angustipes*
sea-snail, common purple	*Janthina janthina*
snail, coffee-bean	*Melampus coffeus*
spirula, common	*Spirula spirula*
star shell, carved	*Astraea caelata*
star shell, green	*A. tuber*
star shell, imbricated	*A. tecta*
star shell, long-spined	*A. phoebia*
tegula, green-base	*Tegula excavata*
top shell, West Indian	*Cittarium pica*
triton, gold-mouthed	*Cymatium nicobaricum*
triton, knobby	*C. muricinum*
triton, trumpet	*Charonia variegata*
tulip shell	*Fasciolaria tulipa*
tunshell, Atlantic partridge	*Tonna maculosa*
turban, chestnut	*Turbo castanea*
vase shell, Nutting's	*Globivasum globulus*
winkle, zebra	*Nodilittorina ziczac*
worm shell, Knorr's	*Vermicularia knorri*

Echinoderms

ophiocoma, spiny	*Ophiocoma echinata*
sea cucumber, Agassiz's	*Actinopyga agassizii*
sea egg, white	*Tripneustes ventricosus*
sea urchin, green rock borer	*Echinometra viridis*
sea urchin, long-spined black	*Diadema antillarum*

sea urchin, pencil	*Eucidris tribuloides*
sea urchin, purple rock borer	*Echinometra lucunter*
sea urchin, six-hole	*Mellita sexiesperforata*
sea urchin, variable	*Lytechinus variegatus*
starfish, two-spined	*Astropecten duplicatus*

Other invertebrates

coral, fire	*Millepora* sp.
jellyfish, upside-down	*Cassiopeia xamachana*
Portuguese man-of-war	*Physalia physalis*
sea anemone, pink-tipped	*Condylactis gigantea*
sea anemone, red warty	*Bunodosoma cavernata*
sea fan, Bahamian	*Gorgonia flabellum*
sea fan, common	*G. ventalina*
sponge, red fire	*Tedania ignis*
tunicate, black	*Ascidia nigra*
tunicate, mangrove	*Eceteinascidia turbinata*
worm, green bristle	*Hermodice carunculata*
worm, orange bristle	*Eurythoe complanata*
worms, mason	A number of worms build such tubes including members of the family Onuphidae
zoanthid, knobby	*Zooanthus pulchellus*
zoanthid, mat	*Palythoa mammillosa*

Reptiles

caiman, spectacled	*Caiman crocodilus*
crocodile, American	*Crocodilus acutus*
four-eye fish	*Anableps* sp.
turtle, green	*Cheloniamydas*
turtle, hawksbill	*Eretmochelys imbricata*
turtle, Kemp's ridley	*Lepidochelys olivacea*
turtle, leatherback	*Dermochelys coriacea*
turtle, loggerhead	*Caretta caretta*
turtle, olive ridley	*Lepidochelys kempi*
boa, tree	*Corallus enydris cookii*

Birds and mammals

booby, brown	*Sula leucogaster*
bullfinch, Lesser Antillean	*Loxigilla noctis*
egret, cattle	*Bubulcus ibis*
egret, common	*Casmerodius albus*
egret, snowy	*Egretta thula*
frigatebird, magnificent	*Fregata magnificens*
grackle, carib	*Quiscalus lugubris*
grackle, Greater Antillean	*Quiscalus niger*
gull, laughing	*Larus atricilla*
heron, green-backed	*Butorides striatus*
heron, little blue	*Egretta caerulea*
heron, yellow crowned night	*Nycticorax violaceus*
ibis, scarlet	*Eudocimus ruber*
oystercatcher, American	*Haematopus palliatus*
pelican, brown	*Pelicanus occidentalis*
plover, semipalmated	*Charadrius semipalmatus*
quit, banana	*Coereba flaveola*
sanderling	*Calidris alba*
sandpiper, spotted	*Actitis macularia*
sloth, two-toed	*Choloepus didactylus*
tern, bridled	*Sterna anaethetus*
tern, royal	*S. maxima*
tern, sandwich	*S. sandvicensis*
tern, sooty	*S. fuscata*
tropicbird, red-billed	*Phaethon aethereus*
tropicbird, white-tailed	*P. lepturus*
turnstone	*Arenaria interpres*
vulture, black	*Coragyps atratus*

Flowering plants including trees

aloe	*Aloe vera*
barringtonia	*Barringtonia asiatica*
bay cedar	*Suriana maritima*
beach knot grass	*Paspalum vaginatum*
beach morning glory	*Ipomoea pes-caprae*
bearded fig	*Ficus citrifolia*
carpet daisy	*Wedelia trilobata*
casuarina	*Casuarina equisetifolia*
century plant	*Agave* sp.

coconut palm	*Cocos nucifera*
columnar cactus	*Pilosocereus royeni*
crab grass	*Sporobolus virginicus*
fat pork	*Chrysobalanus icaco*
manchineel	*Hippomane mancinella*
mangrove, black	*Avicennia germinans*
mangrove, grey	*Conocarpus erectus*
mangrove, red	*Rhizophora mangle*
mangrove, white	*Laguncularia racemosa*
periwinkle	*Catharanthus roseus*
prickly pear	*Opuntia dillenii*
purslane	*Portulaca oleracea*
red wild purslane	*P. pilosa*
rock sage	*Lantana involucrata*
samphire	*Blutaparon vermiculare*
scarlet cordia	*Cordia sebestena*
sea bean	*Canavalia rosea*
sea grape	*Coccoloba uvifera*
sea hibiscus	*Hibiscus tiliaceus*
seaside almond	*Terminalia catappa*
seaside daisy	*Egletes prostrata*
seaside mahoe	*Thespesia populnea*
seaside sage	*Croton flavens*
seaside samphire	*Sesuvium portulacastrum*
small seaside lavender	*Heliotropium curassavicum*
strumpfia	*Strumpfia maritima*
sweet briar	*Acacia tortuosa*
tamarind	*Tamarindus indica*
turks cap cactus	*Melocactus intortus*
turtle grass	*Thalassia testudinum*
yucca	*Yucca aloifolia*

Index

Page numbers in **bold** refer to figures

D

E

F

G

O

P

Q

R

S

T